T0304349

IMAGE TO LIKENESS

Living From The Inside Out

Terry E. Warr

authorHOUSE®

AuthorHouse™
1663 Liberty Drive
Bloomington, IN 47403
www.authorhouse.com
Phone: 1-800-839-8640

First published by AuthorHouse   5/19/2010

ISBN: 978-1-4520-2664-0 (e)
ISBN: 978-1-4520-2662-6 (sc)
ISBN: 978-1-4520-2663-3 (hc)

Library of Congress Control Number: 2010907162

Printed in the United States of America
Bloomington, Indiana

This book is printed on acid-free paper.

This book is dedicated to my lovely wife, Joye L. Warr.

God in His great wisdom knew exactly the kind of wife I needed. I can just imagine Him smiling and laughing the whole time He spent creating you. He put in you everything I would need in a wife. My heart is always overjoyed at the thought of you. You are truly a divine dream come true. You are the most loving, kind, and thoughtful woman I have ever known. You pour your heart and soul into everything you do.

I could not see myself being the man that I am without you in my life. You are my greatest inspiration. Your support always makes me want to be better than I am. I cherish every moment that we share together because you lavish me with the kind of love that every husband desires.

Thank you for loving me the way you do and for letting me take on yet another project in our already busy lives. Let this book be just another reminder to you of my passionate dedication to our covenant of love.

Contents

FORWARD

As I spent time in reflection about the book that you hold in your hands I began to think about the powerful impact that the Bible has on human life. It is not a compilation of books filled with chapters about the lives of individuals aimlessly wandering about without meaning. It is a book filled with wonderful stories about people and relationships - with one another and with God. More often than not, we fail to see ourselves in the pages of these stories. However, until we see our "image" in the stories, they do not hold significant meaning to us. Our greatest obstacle in proper self-image is our lack or inability to understanding God's image. Poor self-image is simply going through life wearing a mask, never really living authentically in His likeness because of the fear that others won't love us if we remove the self-made mask.

For most of my Christian life, I have worn that mask; and often times painfully so. I knew that I needed someone in my life that lived without a mask. I especially desired to have a man of God in my life that knew how to love me where I was in my personal journey and walk with me in genuine and authentic relationship; like the unique relationship that I shared with my deceased father. I needed someone in my life that I could always tell the truth to, someone I could be totally transparent with. But like most men, I, at times found myself subconsciously resisting what I consciously desired. The very first time I met Terry E. Warr, I knew immediately that he was a special anointed vessel of God and that we would share a lifetime friendship. My relationship with him and our mutual friend Melvin Maxwell has truly transformed my life (and I'm still learning) in a way that I can now leave my house without the mask.

In this book Terry will take you on a journey to help you see the bigger picture ... to take the blinders off your eyes so you can discover *your story* within the story. Given that the story is so powerfully captivating and the truths are so inspiring, I believe there are three things that will happen as a result of you reading this book: First, you will feel compelled to read it more than once. Secondly, long after you close the book, the message of the book will not let you go; it will become permanently engrafted in your heart and mind forever. Finally, you will passionately want to share *Image to Likeness* with somebody else.

As a Pastor of a small church and as a CEO, I have always prayed for the tools to effectively share Christ with others. Terry has written a book that is bound to be a Christian classic for future generations, but the book is also brilliantly written in a way that will allow you to share God's uncommon and unconditional love with others. He takes the mystery out of the message and allows the reader to say, *"I finally get it. There's more to me than the image in the mirror!"*

Just when I thought I understood God's love, *Image to Likeness* came along and took God's love to a deeper level than I could ever imagine. This book will not only give you a greater appreciation for who you are, but it will also give you a greater appreciation for other people and for God.

I strongly suggest that you read this book from cover to cover and by all means participate in the i2L challenge at the conclusion of the book.

Dr. Dwight McKinney Senior Pastor
Manifested Life Community Fellowship
Hawthorne, CA

Chapter 1

IN A STATE OF SHOCK

Shocked! I guess that is the best way to describe it. Shocked and scared to death. Yes, the shock and fear eventually subsided, but initially I was terrified.

Your first reaction may be that I am crazy. I'm not. I don't even like spooky stuff, but what I am about to share with you really happened, and it has changed my life forever.

I was told to share with each of you what I learned and to offer you this promise: if you apply the principles in this book, you too will experience miraculous things in your journey—things that you have never imagined. I hope you are ready for this, because to tell the truth, I wasn't when it all happened to me.

Darkness greeted me as I frantically awakened from a deep sleep. The beeping of a menacing alarm was the culprit. I could see the green light surrounding the numbers 5:00 on the clock as I reached to silence it and grab my glasses. My pants and shirt finally made their way onto my slow-moving, groggy body. I pushed my feet into my Jordan sneakers, grabbed my bag, and walked to my cold SUV, reminding myself why I was doing these unnatural early-morning workouts.

The trip to the gym takes about ten minutes, and it's during this time that I reflect on the direction of my life. This recurring contemplative act can be paralyzing at times. It's not like I'm unhappy, but something seemed to be missing in my life. Most of the questions floating around in my head on this particular morning were provoked by a passage of scripture I had been studying. I have read it hundreds of times, but for some reason, this time it snatched my consciousness and bent it into submission. It just would not let go.

Genesis 1:26–27 says that *God created us in His image and in His likeness.* Wow! What does that really mean? Question after question kept rolling out of my mind like an assembly line.

- *How does God define likeness, and how does it apply to my life?*
- *Is my resemblance to God physical? Is it spiritual? Is it emotional?*
- *What does God really expect of me?*
- *Is my life an accident or an incident?*
- *Why am I even here on earth, and what difference am I making?*

I could not stop myself. I wondered if I was the man God wanted me to be. Was there something missing in me or in the experiences that shaped me? I rationalized that I was a good person. I was a good father. I was a committed husband. I worked hard every day. I got along with the people in my life. But I still felt something was missing in my life. I didn't have a real sense of who I was. I knew deep within my heart that I was experiencing an identity crisis.

During my workout, I was oblivious to my sets and routine. I kept pondering all those questions and others. On my way home from the gym, I missed my normal turns and almost stomped a hole through my car from last-second braking. In fact all morning long, as I helped my family prepare for the day, I was completely distracted. I was going through the motions, but I was deep in thought the whole time. I couldn't stop thinking about all of the things that weren't quite right in my life. The more I thought, the more frustrated I became. I saw my family off with a blank stare.

Right after my wife and children left the house, I began to get ready for a day at the office. Nothing out of the ordinary. I squeezed the last of the toothpaste and brushed my teeth, showered in piping hot water, and was about to shave when the craziest thing I have ever experienced happened. The image in the mirror—my spitting image—began to talk to me. Yes, you read it right! No, you don't have to read it again. I know it sounds crazy, but that is what happened. You cannot imagine how terrified I was.

My mouth dropped to the floor as I slowly wiped off the steam from the other half of the mirror with my elbow. Every muscle in my body tensed up as the razor fell from my hand into the water. I almost rubbed my eyes out of the sockets hoping the talking image would disappear. Several thoughts ran through my mind as fast as a speeding bullet. At first I thought I was dreaming. Then I thought I was losing my mind. Then I didn't know what to think. Meanwhile, as if "he" expected my puzzled response, my image calmly waited until it appeared that I had gained my composure.

Then he said, "I know my visit has come as a surprise to you."

"That's the understatement of the year," I thought.

Still in a state of shock, I mumbled, "This can't be real. I am looking in the mirror at myself talking to me."

"That's right," he said. "And before you lose your mind, let me explain a few things. I have been sent to you by Dad—the one you call God. He has sent me here to help you understand who you are and what you can accomplish in your life. I am here to help you learn to live from the inside out."

"What do you mean 'live from the inside out'? What are you talking about?" I asked.

"There is more to you than meets the eye," he explained. "Whenever you look in the mirror, I know you only expect to see your image, but your image reflects only how you look on the outside. There is so much more to you than your physical appearance. There is more to you than the mirror can show you. If you are like most people, there is a good chance that you have bought into the notion that mirrors don't lie. But

I am here to tell you that mirrors do lie. They tell you half-truths, which are nothing more than lies. They never reveal who you are on the inside. I am here to take you beyond the ordinary limits of the mirror. I am here to expose you to an internal mirror that fully reveals the essence of who you really are. I am here to introduce you to the person that Dad designed you to be."

As the image spoke, I just stood there mesmerized. His words made sense, but my mind wasn't ready to fully embrace what was happening.

The image continued. "In the life you are currently living, you have three options. The first option is to *be a wanderer.* This option is the easiest because it requires no action at all. Essentially all you have to do is keep going through the motions day in and day out until your life is over. You can choose to be like the people who live until they are a ripe old age but die on the inside when they were very young. They just wander through life haphazardly without any clear purpose or direction.

"The second option is to *allow the world around you to dictate your identity and the outcome of your life.* If you select this option, you will live your life relying on others for your success and happiness. You will surrender your hopes and dreams into the hands of others and become a victim of their desires.

"And the third option is to *discover your real identity and become who Dad created you to be.* If you select this option, you will live life with purpose, passion, and power. You will face life's challenges with a confident assurance that enables you to overcome anything. You will discover things about yourself that will amaze you.

"Most people live their lives at either option one or option two. They do nothing, or they let the world around them control their lives. Very few ever reach the place of promise by intentionally living their lives from the inside out.

"You need to know that even with my help you can still choose whatever option you want," he continued.

Then he said something that was simple, yet profound. (Actually he did that a lot, but for some reason his next few statements hit me like a bolt of lightning.) "One of the greatest gifts Dad has given you is the power to choose. This gives you power to live beyond what is happening around you. Many people allow their situations or circumstances to dictate their lives. But the power to choose allows you to rise above any and every circumstance and situation in your life. You may not be able to choose what happens to you, but you can always choose your response. Always remember and never forget: You have the power to choose. Good health is a choice. Bad health is a choice. Wealth is a choice. Poverty is a choice. Love is a choice. Hatred is a choice. Faith is a choice. Faithlessness is a choice. Never underestimate the power of choice."

The look on his face was intense. His right eyebrow was slightly raised, and there was a noticeable wrinkle in the middle of his forehead. "Let's be clear from the very beginning: There is one catch, and it is a very important one. You must be willing to share the knowledge I teach you with the rest of the world."

Even after listening to his explanation, I was thinking, "This is way too crazy for me. Nobody is going to believe this. I am having a hard time believing it myself. I have got to be dreaming." I was about to hyperventilate. Once again I rubbed my eyes, hoping to regain the vision I thought I might have lost.

Still in disbelief, I asked, "Are you someone out of the Bible or something? I mean, you certainly look like me...but none of this makes sense."

He said, "I know this doesn't make any sense right now, but it will in a few minutes. I don't want you to major in the minors. Instead of wondering who I am, I want you to focus on who you are. I don't want you to completely miss the point."

"What point? Do you realize that I am standing in the mirror talking to someone who looks like me, but who apparently isn't me? This is a mirror, for crying out loud. You are supposed to be a mere reflection of me, not a separate being. In fact, I can't believe I am still standing here talking to myself...or to you."

"I know this is hard for you. I also know this is out of the ordinary. But if you want extraordinary things, you have to be willing to step outside of ordinary situations. "

5

I was beginning to get it. Now I knew how some of the people in the Bible felt when they received a divine visitation. "What is your name?" I asked, trying to regain my composure.

"My name?" he replied. "We have the same name. I am you, remember."

I said, "Yes, I know, but this is still quite confusing."

"Okay. I tell you what: If it will simplify things for you, call me Likeness."

Something about his name really resonated with me. Although my mind was still a bit foggy, I realized something profound was about to take place.

"Okay. I'll call you Likeness."

"Great. Now let's get on with what I have come here to do," Likeness said. "First we need to solidify our agreement. Do you agree to share the knowledge I am about to teach you with the rest of the world?"

By now, I was beginning to come back to my normal self. I still felt a little awkward, but my fear was subsiding.

"Uh...yes...yes, I do." I agreed to his request, even though I wasn't really sure what it meant. "I promise I will share what you teach me with the rest of the world. In a strange kind of way, I am excited about what lies ahead."

Likeness smiled. "The first thing I am going to do is teach you about who you really are in Dad's eyes." He twisted his hands together as though he were anxious to get started.

Likeness continued referring to God as Dad. I must admit that I was a little uncomfortable with that term. Calling Him Father was more acceptable because it felt a little more formal.

I finally asked, "Why do you keep calling God Dad?"

"Because that's who He is," Likeness replied. "You call Him God, and occasionally you refer to Him as Father or Lord, but I call Him Dad all the time because I fully understand my relationship with Him."

"Are you saying I don't fully understand my relationship with Him?"

"I'm sorry. I don't mean to offend you. Your understanding of the One you call God is growing, and therefore your awareness of who He is grows also. Eventually you will see that He is Dad, plain and simple.

"You need to fully understand some things about Dad that are important if you are going to experience all that He has in store for you. So you need to listen very carefully. As a matter of fact, you will need a notebook so that you can have a written record of everything you learn during our time together."

Out of nowhere, a purple pen and a blue-and-white notebook appeared on the marble counter directly in front of me.

"Will you please tell me a few seconds in advance before you start materializing notebooks and pens out of thin air?" My tone was sharper than I intended, but the sudden appearance of these items caught me off guard. "This is my first conversation with the mirror, and it takes some adjustment. Making stuff appear out of thin air is a little too much for me right now."

Likeness's loud and hearty laughter filled the room. The sound of it was the same as my own laughter. "I apologize. Dad does things like that from time to time, and I've gotten used to it, but I can imagine how you feel. This notebook will assist you in recording our experience together. It is thought-, event-, and voice-activated."

"What do you mean?"

"It is really quite simple. It accurately records our interaction and your thoughts on its own. It makes your job very easy. All you have to do is be who you are, and it will record everything."

I picked up the notebook and looked inside. Just as Likeness said, it had already recorded our brief exchange and my thoughts from earlier in the day.

"This is crazy! I really must be losing my mind."

"You are not losing your mind. Whether you are aware of it or not, everything you say, think, and do is always being recorded. Dad doesn't miss a thing. He knows every little detail there is to know about you. In fact, He has even numbered every hair on your head."

Because I was beginning to go bald, I said, "Yes, and He must know that there a few numbers of hair missing. I think numbers 12 through 20 aren't there anymore, and 30 through 40 aren't either." We both laughed like old friends.

"That is funny. I love your sense of humor." Likeness cleared his throat and got back to business. "Dad is into details. He has numbered every hair on your head. Not only does He know how many hairs there are, but He also knows which numbers are missing. And by the way, your numbers are off. The accurate missing numbers are 14 through 40 and 60 and above," he chuckled.

I laughed, and the lightheartedness of the moment put me at ease.

Likeness continued, "Think of it this way. This notebook introduces you to technology from eternity. It is no different from the gadgets you are used to in your world. It's just a lot more advanced. Besides, if it makes you feel any better, I will ask you to write a few things in the book later on during our time together. But for now, accept it as a gift to help you record our experience so you will be able to share what you learn with others."

"Okay, I guess it is just taking me some time to get used to all of that is happening."

"You are doing fine. You are handling everything very well. Now let's get going," Likeness urged.

"Where are we going?"

"You'll see..."

IMAGE

Then God said, "Let us make man in our image."
(Gen 1:26 NIV)
"Image represents form and can never be changed!"

Chapter 2

OUR IDENTITY CRISIS

The bathroom scene and my clothing began to change. "Maybe I'm not as ready as I thought," I mused.

The mirror disappeared. The marble countertop and sink vanished. I was no longer dressed in my bathrobe. Instead I found myself fully dressed in denim slacks and a white, short-sleeved shirt. So many things were happening around me at the same time that it was difficult for me to keep up with the changing landscape. It was as if we were standing in the eye of a storm. Brilliant colors swirled all around us. I could hear the sound of rushing wind circling us, yet neither of us was affected by its apparent power. It all happened so quickly that I didn't have time for fear. I was too fascinated to be afraid. In fact, in a strange kind of way, I felt like a newborn baby experiencing life for the very first time.

Likeness was standing directly in front of me. When I finally looked at him, his smile assured me that everything was fine. Just as Likeness and I made eye contact, the wind subsided and the swirling colors that had engulfed us settled down into a metropolitan landscape. We found ourselves right in the middle of a concrete jungle. The noises of the big city suddenly came rushing in like a flood. Car horns were blowing, people were talking, and the subway rumbled in the distance. I could feel the warmth of the summer sun beaming down upon my face. The air was thick with humidity and the smell of hotdogs cooking. The place was not familiar to me, but Likeness appeared to be right at home.

He began, "I brought you here to show you something."

"Brought me where?"

"Where you are is not important. What is important is what you have come to learn. In a few minutes, you are going to meet four different people. Observe them closely. Each one of them is going to engage you in a brief, one-on-one conversation. My only involvement will be to let you know when it is time for you to move to the next person. At the end of this encounter, you and I will talk about what you have observed."

"What is the purpose for doing this?"

"I want to teach you something about how and why people see themselves the way that they do. By the way, the first person has just spotted you."

I turned around, but I didn't see anyone. I turned back around and asked, "Who are..." but Likeness was gone. "I must be crazy," I muttered.

"Who must be crazy?" asked the woman standing directly behind me.

She startled me and I whirled around abruptly. I saw a middle-aged white woman standing with a shopping cart full of clothes, plastic bags, and pots and pans. She was obviously a bag lady. Her clothes were tattered and torn. Her hair was matted and nappy, but her teeth and skin were absolutely beautiful. In fact I don't remember ever seeing teeth as straight and white as hers or skin quite so smooth. I could smell liquor on her breath.

"Are you calling me crazy"? she asked.

"No, I was talking to myself."

"Oh, so you do that too? I thought I was the only one who called myself crazy. For twenty-seven years I have been told I was crazy; now I am beginning to believe it. But I am here to tell you that you'd better be careful. You know what the Good Book says, don't you?"

"Good Book?"

"Yeah, the Good Book. The Bible, Silly. It says that 'life and death are in the power of the tongue.' If you keep telling yourself you are crazy, before too long, you'll begin to believe it. But you don't have to listen to me. *I am nobody! I am just an old bag lady with a drinking problem.*"

As we walked along, I decided to ask her a few questions.

"How long have you been living on the street?"

She began to spew out one question after another. "Who told you that I am living on the street? Is it that obvious? Don't I look respectable enough to live somewhere other than the street? Why are you talking to me in the first place? You must be crazy because no one ever talks to me."

"No, I am not crazy. I am just trying to..."

"Trying to what? Trying to hurt me? That is what people do best—hurt other people. Well, I refuse to be hurt ever again."

She must be suffering from some type of mental disorder, I thought.

She picked up her pace and began to walk slightly ahead of me. Then as though she had forgotten something very important, she stopped and turned to face me. I didn't know what to expect. "By the way, do you have any loose change so I can get me a nip?" she asked.

I was just about to answer her when Likeness walked up and gave her a big hug, kissed her on the cheek, whispered something in her ear, and gave her a handful of money. She smiled and rushed off in haste. Why did he give her all of that money, I wondered. Didn't he know that she was... In the middle of my thought, I heard Likeness speaking.

"The second person is right behind you."

I turned around to see who it was, but once again nobody was there. When I turned back around, Likeness was gone. "This doesn't make any sense," I complained.

A voice behind me asked, "What doesn't make any sense?"

I turned around and saw a Korean gentleman who appeared to be in his mid-thirties. He was very well groomed, with a jet black mustache and a thick, well-trimmed beard. He looked very distinguished in wire-rimmed sunglasses, jeans, and a white tee shirt printed with the words "I am proud to be a Korean American." Around his neck was a very lovely gold cross with a beautiful birthstone in the middle. He was standing in front of me rubbing his hands together as though he were very nervous or upset.

I responded, "It's nothing. I am..."

He interrupted me. "Are you a Christian?"

"Yes, I am." Then I thought, "Whatever happened to 'Hi, my name is...?"

"Can I ask you a question"?

"Sure go right ahead."

"Is it wrong for a Korean to marry a Latina?"

I was a little taken aback by his question, but I replied, "No, I don't think it's wrong. Why do you ask?"

"I want to marry a young lady who goes to my church. We really love one another, but she is Latina and I am Korean."

"So what's the problem? I don't..." Before I could finish my sentence he continued.

"I wasn't born in this country. I came to America with my parents when I was four years old. All I have ever known is America. My parents are traditional and a bit old-fashioned. They are good parents and all, but their views send me mixed signals. They raised me as a Christian, yet they are totally against me marrying someone outside of our nationality. They say I will be a disgrace to the family if I marry my fiancée who happens to be a Latina. I don't want to disgrace my Korean heritage, but as a Christian I feel it is perfectly okay for me to marry my fiancée. The Bible teaches that in Christ we all are equal and there should be no division, but obviously my parents feel differently. I don't know what to do. *To tell you the truth, I don't know who I am anymore...* Listen, I'm sorry I bothered you with this. There is no way you could ever understand. You are not Korean. Thanks for listening, though."

And with that he took off walking down the street.

I mumbled, "Nice talking to you. I hope things work out for you."

Likeness appeared alongside me.

"Some chatterbox, huh?" he commented. "It seems our brother had a lot on his mind. I am sure you learned a lot in a very short time. Sometimes in a big city people don't really talk *to* each other; they talk *at* each other. Don't take it personally. It's something that has become a part of big city living."

"Yeah I guess you are right," I replied. "Whenever I am upset about something, I tend to do the same thing."

We began walking, and for the first time, I noticed that big-city life was in full swing. All up and down the street were shoeshine stands, hot dog stands, break dancers, and musicians. An Oriental woman was doing neck and shoulder massages. Likeness put some money in the basket of every vendor we passed. I was just about to ask him why he did that when he blurted out, "I love the big city! There are so many fascinating people here. In fact, you are about to meet one of them right now."

By now I knew the drill: I would look, and Likeness would disappear. This time, however, Likeness walked over to a young man selling paintings and began a conversation with him. I couldn't hear what he was saying because his back was turned to me. I was about to join them when someone tapped me on the back. I turned around and saw an African American lady.

Immediately I noticed that there was something special about her. She was a naturally beautiful woman. She had beautiful brown eyes and a rich dark brown complexion. Her high cheekbones made her look very regal, and her nose and lips were picture perfect. She was about 5′ 6″, and she had an attractive shape. But after that everything got a little weird. Her blond wig did not seem to fit the shape of her face, and she wore way too much makeup. Her rich burgundy dress was cut too low in the front, revealing more of her body than anyone needed to see. She had very long fake designer fingernails and stood with her hands folded in front of her. The gray leather shoulder bag draped over her right shoulder perfectly matched her shoes.

"This woman would be beautiful if she took off all of that fake stuff," I thought.

"Excuse me, Sir," she said. "I seem to have lost my way, and I am in need of your guidance."

Her choice of words and articulation were a surprise to me. She appeared to be fairly educated. It was delightful to finally meet someone who appeared to be somewhat polite.

"Oh, I'm sorry, but I'm not from around here. Where are you trying to go? Maybe you can ask one of the street vendors."

"I am looking for Agape Movie Studios. I have an audition in a few hours, and I wanted to get to the studio early."

"Oh, so you are an actress?"

"Well, I want to be. I moved here hoping to launch my acting career. I have been auditioning for parts now for about four years with no success."

"Yeah, I can only imagine that launching an acting career is not easy. If you don't mind me asking—what do you think the problem has been?

"Well, it is not my acting. I have been told countless times that my acting is great. But *they say* I don't "look" the part. Most of the good parts go to women who...let's just say they don't look like me. *So I have been trying different looks to see if I can fit in. To be quite honest with you, I think I am starting to lose myself in the process.* Sir, I am sorry. I really didn't mean to burden you with my problems. I'll take your advice and ask one of the street vendors. I really should be going."

"Oh, it's no problem. It was really good talking to you. I hope today's audition will be just right for you."

She said, "Thanks!" and walked a few steps up the street to get directions from one of the street vendors The next thing I knew, Likeness was back at my side once again. We continued walking down the street. He said, "Our sister was a wonderful person, wasn't she?"

"Yes, she was. I really wanted to talk with her a little longer. As I listened to her story, I got a sense that there was a possibility I could help her find her way."

"There is a good possibility that you will help her in due time," Likeness responded. "But for now you will need to concentrate on the assignment at hand. Your next exchange is only seconds away."

I was really beginning to enjoy these brief encounters, especially in light of the fact that they were a part of this whole fascinating experience with Likeness. I wasn't sure why I was learning what I was learning, but I knew at some point all of this had to make sense, so I readied myself for my next encounter.

Likeness and I had reached one of the largest intersections I had ever seen. There were four lanes of traffic going in both directions. As we stood at the crosswalk waiting for the light to change, Likeness decided to patronize one of the young men shining shoes. He walked over, grabbed a newspaper, and sat down.

Just then I heard someone behind me say the words, "This is just disgusting!"

I turned around to see who it was and saw a white gentleman who appeared to be in his mid-fifties. He looked like a corporate executive. He had sandy gray hair, bushy eyebrows, and a clean-shaven face. He was dressed to the hilt in a dark blue double-breasted silk suit, a white tailor-made shirt with his initials on the right cuff, a bright red silk tie, and a pocket square to match.

I took a chance and initiated the conversation. "What is disgusting?"

"Excuse me?" he replied.

"You just said something was disgusting. I'm just curious about what you are referring to."

"There are way too many vendors on the street these days. That's what is disgusting. These people are just beggars. That is no way for a person to make a living. Why don't these people get real jobs? My limo driver can't see where I am standing because there are too many people out here."

"What's wrong with earning a living as a street vendor?"

"Listen, I know that *money makes a man* and that every man should do his best to take care of his household, but working for the few pennies these people make is a total waste of time."

Instead of creating an argument by defending the street vendors, I decided to find out more about him. "Do you work around here?" I inquired.

"I guess you can say that. Do you see that tall glass building?" He pointed to a building a few yards away.

"Yes, I see it."

"I own it. I employ over five hundred people, and I have offices all over the world. Why do you ask? Are you looking for a job? You aren't a street vendor, are you?"

"No, Sir, I'm not. I'm just a visitor here. I guess you have done very well for yourself."

"I guess you can say that *I am a self-made millionaire.* Right now I am late for an important meeting and here comes my limo. Good-bye."

"Good-bye, Sir."

At that moment a black Cadillac limousine pulled up, and the driver ran around the car to open the rear door for the corporate executive. The driver was very well groomed with a full beard cut close to his face and well-manicured hands. He looked a little out of place. Although I did not know him, there was something different about him. He apologized profusely for not being able to spot his boss. He ran back around to the driver side, looked at me over the top of the car, winked and gave me thumbs up, jumped in the car, and drove off.

"I would hate to have him as a boss," I thought. "He is a cold, cruel, and selfish man."

I walked over to the shoeshine stand where Likeness was just wrapping up his business with the attendant. Likeness looked at me and said, "The beloved brother you spoke to was really a magnificent man, wasn't he?"

"I wouldn't exactly call him magnificent. He was full of himself."

Likeness chuckled. "Okay, observation time is over. Now let's get down to the fun part!"

"What fun part?"

"You'll see!"

Chapter 3

AN INSIDE LOOK

The landscape changed once again—without all of the drama and fanfare the last time. As soon as I turned my head, we were alone in a classroom setting. Several things reminded me of our first encounter. The mirror and the marble countertop were exactly the same. I was seated on a very comfortable stool facing the mirror. Likeness was "in" the mirror, and what appeared to be a large blackboard consumed the entire background. The lighting in the room was extremely bright, but I could not tell where the light came from. Likeness began to walk back and forth with his hands folded behind his back.

He said, "For this next stage of learning, it is important that we remove all distractions, so I thought a little change of scenery would be in order. As you can see, I borrowed a few elements from our first encounter. I wanted you to feel at home. And besides, I just love this mirror; it makes me look thin."

Likeness's sudden sense of humor threw me off guard. He chuckled and I laughed.

As he continued to pace back and forth, he said, "I have chosen to use this mirror as a teaching tool. Since we are dealing with the idea of image, I want this mirror to remind you of two important points. First, you are more than what you can see with your natural vision. People put way too much emphasis on physical appearances. Don't get me wrong;

physical appearance has its importance. But physical appearance should not be emphasized over and above what's in your heart.

Second, we were all formed to be a reflection of someone much greater than ourselves. Always remember and never forget: We did not make ourselves, and therefore we are ill equipped to define ourselves. We will talk more about this point as we go further along. The blank canvas behind me is also a teaching tool that will be used at the appropriate time to help your learning experience. Are you with me so far?"

"Yes, I am, but I do have one question."

"What is that?"

"Where is the bright light coming from? This place is awfully bright!"

"Ah, yes, the light. I really didn't notice it myself because my eyes have already adjusted to it. The light that you see means that you are growing to another level of spiritual understanding. You are slowly coming out of darkness into Dad's marvelous light. Don't worry. The more you live what you learn, the more your eyes will adjust."

"I can't wait!"

"Great! Let's go over what you observed. You had brief encounters with four different people. As we review each one, I want you to tell me what you saw on the outside, and I will tell you what was happening on the inside."

"Well, in the encounter with the bag lady, several things leaped out at me. Her beautiful teeth and smooth, radiant skin made me think that at one time she had taken good care of herself."

"That is a great observation. Prior to her current situation, she has always been an attractive woman who took good care of herself."

"The next thing that was a bit odd to me was her age. She was twenty-seven years old. That's way too young to be a bag lady."

"Oh, is there a bag lady minimum age requirement that I don't know about?"

"Well, you know what I mean."

"No, I don't. Please tell me."

"Most bag ladies I have seen are in their fifties or older."

"And?"

"What I am trying to say is that twenty-seven is such a young age to end up as a bag lady."

"I agree."

"Anyway, the next thing I noticed was that she was an alcoholic. For some reason she drank a lot. Finally, I noticed that she had a mental problem. She thought I was going to hurt her when in fact my intentions were to help her."

"Is there anything else?"

"No, nothing that I can think of."

"You made several wonderful observations. I can see that you were very alert. I want to draw your attention to a few other points. Do you remember the words she spoke during your exchange?"

"Oh yeah, now I remember. She said, 'Life and death are in the power of the tongue.' She also said that she has been told she is crazy for twenty-seven years and now she is starting to believe it. In addition, she said that all people do is hurt people and she would never let herself get hurt again."

"Do you also remember how she identified herself?"

"Yeah. She said she was nobody. She called herself 'an old bag lady with a drinking problem.' Which reminds me, why did you give her a handful of money? Didn't you know she would use it to buy alcohol?"

"I knew you would ask that question. I will answer it in just a minute, but for now let me share with you what was happening on the inside of her—mentally and emotionally.

"The precious young lady you met has come to see herself through the eyes of pain. When she was a young girl, her father abandoned her and her mother for his gay lover. She was only seven at the time, and she blamed herself for the divorce. She thought that if she had been a better daughter, her mom and dad would have stayed together. Nothing could be further from the truth, but to her, her perception was reality. After her parents' divorce, her mom had to take on a second job, leaving little to no time for her. Because of the divorce, she essentially lost the love and guidance of both parents. Her mother's absence, coupled with the loss of her father, made the pain of her family life much worse.

"Through trial and error, she learned how to fend for herself. For twenty years, she suffered through several unhealthy relationships in an attempt to find love and affirmation. During that twenty-year period, she was only able to find true friendship with one young lady. They have been friends since elementary school. Three years ago she met and fell in love with her fiancé. The pain of her life became too much to bear when she came home one evening and found her fiancé and best friend sexually involved with one another two days before her scheduled wedding!

"The mental and emotional anguish became the straw that broke the camel's back. Her head and heart were racked with pain, and in an instant, pain had the potential to shape the rest of her life! She completely abandoned life as she knew it. She tried to medicate her pain with alcohol and took up residence on the streets. Slowly but surely, she became more and more secure in her new identity. Her mental and emotional reasoning is that it is safer to push people away than to deal with the pain of constant disappointment."

"Wow! I guess we can't always judge a book by its cover."

"You are right. We should never judge anyone solely by what we see, although we do it every day."

"I still don't understand why you gave her the money."

"First, I didn't just give her money. I gave her money with a purpose in mind."

"What do you mean?"

"I'll answer your question with a question. Why wouldn't *you* give her money?"

"Because I knew she was an alcoholic."

"That is exactly right. You labeled her an alcoholic. You wouldn't give her money because of who you thought she was. But I gave her money because I know who she is. When you looked at her, you saw an alcoholic bag lady. But when I look at her, I see someone who has been created in the image of our Dad and is temporarily deceived by

23

pain and persuaded by fear. So what you would not do based on her current situation, I did because I knew her situation was temporary. Your evaluation was hopeless. My evaluation was hopeful. I knew she was greater than her circumstances, but you thought her circumstances defined her. Your assessment of her was rooted in her outer appearance, while my assessment is rooted in a part of her that only Dad can see. I gave her money because I knew she had to discover on her own that what she needed was not going to be found in alcohol. Okay, enough about her. Let's move on to your second encounter."

"My second encounter was with the distinguished-looking Korean American gentleman. I remember him being well groomed, although he did seem a bit anxious and impolite. He was obviously wrestling between his Christian orientation and his cultural heritage. It seemed that he wanted to honor both without dishonoring either one. He loved and respected his parents, but he also wanted to marry his Latina fiancée. He was really in a quandary."

"Yes, he was. The reason he was in a quandary was that he primarily saw himself through the eyes of his earthly parents. In other words, his identity or image was tied primarily to his cultural heritage. He wanted to honor his father and his mother, but honoring them appeared to be in direct conflict with his relationship with Dad and his relationship with his fiancée. He said he didn't know who he was anymore. He was wavering between two opinions. Under the circumstances, what should he do?"

"He should embrace his relationship with God over his relationship with his parents," I replied.

"That is easier said than done, don't you think?"

"Yes, it is."

"Why do you suppose it is?"

"Because our parents are our primary caregivers."

"You are right. They are the ones who teach you just about everything during your formative years. You learn about hygiene, nutrition, relationships, finances, religion, cultural heritage, political views, sports, time management, responsibility, physical fitness, education, etc. from your parents. Habits are formed, ingrained messages are deeply rooted, and generational patterns are established during those years.

"Parenting is very important to the overall growth and development of every child. The problem comes when the parents fail to parent their children according to Dad's design. According to Dad's Family Book of Wisdom—the book you call the Bible—Dad instructs parents to teach their children about Him as one of the primary responsibilities of parenting. But way too often parents fail in this responsibility. As a result, the children end up estranged from Dad and depend solely on their earthly parents for their identity. Family identity is important, but it should be secondary to our identity with Dad."

Likeness paused from his pacing directly in front of me and said, "I want to let you in on a little secret."

"What's that?" I asked.

"Do you know why Dad arranged it so that children look like their parents?"

"No. Please tell me why."

"As a reminder to us all that we are made in His image. Every time you see a child who looks like his or her parents, it should serve as a reminder that we are made in our Dad's image."

"Wow! I never thought of our family resemblances quite like that."

"All of creation begins and ends with Him! Where was I? Oh yeah, I was talking about parental influence. The underlying factors that greatly affect the relationships between parents and children are the mental and emotional connections that are established between them during the early years of development. If parental influence is firmly established, it is often difficult to introduce another influence into the life of the child."

"Are you saying that children can only be influenced by their parents?"

"No! Children can be influenced by friends, other family members, the media, teachers, classmates, etc. The possibilities are endless. What I am saying is that parents play a significant role as primary influencers.

If they do an effective job, outside influences become *difficult* but not *impossible*. Parental influence should progressively decrease as children grow to maturity, but many times parental influence is just as active during adulthood as it was during childhood."

"That is so true. I know several people who told me that they vowed never to be like their parents, only to discover later in life that they are just like them!"

"I have seen the same thing. As adults you aren't always aware of parental influences in your lives because they are so deeply entrenched. It is only during critical or stressful times that these dormant influences rise to the surface. In the case of our Korean American brother, his parental influences had him in a very uncomfortable place. His head and heart were in conflict with one another. Logically he knew what he had to do: embrace his Christianity and marry his fiancée. But emotionally it was difficult to execute! His love for his parents and his Korean heritage certainly weighed heavy on his heart."

"I would hate to be in his shoes."

"You will soon discover that you and he are sharing the same shoes."

"What do you mean?"

"You'll find out soon enough, but for now let's talk about your next encounter."

"Okay. My third encounter was with a very polite and articulate African American woman. She was really a very naturally beautiful young lady. She had gorgeous eyes and chocolate brown skin. Her facial features made her look very regal. But her attire was a bit too revealing for my taste, and I had a sense that it wasn't to her liking either. She wore way too much makeup, and her blond wig didn't suit her at all. I remember thinking how attractive she would be if she took off all of the fake stuff. She shared with me that she had been doing auditions for four years with no success. She said she was a great actress, but she didn't seem to fit in with the status quo. So in an attempt to land a part in a film, she was trying different looks. She said she felt she was losing herself in the process. She didn't appear to be happy at all."

"Yes, you are right. She wasn't happy at all. Mentally and emotionally, she had completely given up. At this point in her life, she was simply going through the motions. She saw herself through the eyes of other people. She was trying desperately to please the public. She said all of the good parts went to woman who didn't look like her. She placed a higher premium on what others thought of her than what she thought of herself. She hated the fact that she wasn't accepted for who she was, but she reasoned that she would do whatever it took to make her dream of an acting career come true.

"Her attire was an outward display of an inward loathing in her heart. Slowly but surely, she was starting to hate herself for not being something other than what she was. In her mind she wasn't what 'they' wanted, and so being who she was prevented her from having what she wanted. And do you know the sad part? If she knew who she really was, she could have more than she ever imagined."

"You know, I had the same thought. Do you remember I told you that I wanted to talk to her a little longer because I felt I could help her?"

"Yes, I remember."

"I wanted to tell her right then and there that she was naturally beautiful. All she had to do was to take off all of that fake stuff and be who she was."

"Hold your horses, my brother. That is all well and good. But your approach, while it is noble, would have been the wrong approach. You see, the problem was deeper than the makeup and the fake stuff. The problem was on the inside. You are concerned with style. The problem isn't style; it is substance. It wasn't enough just to tell her to be who she was. She needed to understand who she was before she could be who she was."

"What do you mean?"

"It will be plain to you very soon, but first..."

"I know. I know. Let's go on to the next encounter."

Likeness joined his hands together in front of him, slightly bowed several times, and said, "Very good, Grasshopper. Very good."

"Grasshopper?"

"Oh, don't tell me you never watched *Kung Fu* with David Carradine."

We both broke out in harmonious laughter.

I said, "Likeness, you are funnnnny!"

"I told you, when I get rolling, watch out!" Still smiling, he said, "Please, let's talk about your last exchange."

I chuckled a few more times and said, "Okay. The last person I met was a corporate executive. He was a middle-aged white male, and he was sharp as a tack. He had on a blue double-breasted silk suit, a white tailor-made shirt, and a red tie with a pocket square to match. He was very demeaning toward the street vendors. He said that it was disgusting to have so many street vendors on the street. He also said they should all go and get 'real jobs.' He told me that money makes a man. Then he made it a point to show me the building he owned and to tell me about the number of employees he has, his offices all over the world, his limousine, and the fact that he was a 'self-made millionaire.' He was arrogant, proud, and belittling."

"Yes, he was. He saw himself through the eyes of his possessions. He lived in a world of competition and comparisons. His sense of worth is tied to what he owns, the amount of money he has, the size of his limo, and the number of people he employs. He thinks anyone who has less than he does is not in his league. Belittling others makes him feel superior to them. He feels powerful because of his money. Not only is his identity tied to it, but so is his security. He is cold and calculating.

"He thinks everybody wants what he has, so he spends most of his time trying to protect himself from the people around him. He trusts no one and as a result has no genuine friendships. His blessing has become a curse to him. The very thing he should use to help others, he uses only to isolate himself. His paranoia has led to bitterness because he finds it hard to enjoy the normalcy of everyday life. He is struggling with all of these internal issues because he sees himself through the eyes of his possessions. He has become an island unto himself with no tourist activity."

"Wow! After hearing what is happening on the inside of this man, I guess it is safe to say that what appeared to be polished on the outside was really painful on the inside."

"I don't think I could have said it better myself. Now that you have completed your first assignment, let me explain the significance of what you have just learned. Do you remember earlier when I told you about the power to choose?"

"Yes. You said that one of the greatest gifts Dad has given us is the power to choose."

"That's right. Now let me take that truth a step further. The greatest choice you will ever make is your identity. Here is the critical question: Who or what is going to shape your life? In other words, whose image are you going to embrace as your true identity? I have shared four options: pain, people, parents, and possessions. You are faced with each one of these options every day. In fact, the reason I chose these options is the powerful impact they have in the lives of most people. Any one can easily allow one or more of these options to become defining factors in their lives. Take a few minutes to think about it. Can you identify areas in your life when one or more of these options has attempted to define your existence?"

"Now that you mention it, yes, I can. When it comes to pain, disappointing relationships from my past have caused me to be less trusting of people. It also makes me less willing to go out of my way to help people. From time to time I have a tendency to be a people pleaser. I want everyone to like me, so I compromise in certain areas. I know there are places of tension between my earthly parental influence and my heavenly parental instructions. One quick example is the idea of loving your enemies. We weren't taught to love our enemies growing up. Enemies were to be dealt with in an adversarial manner. Come to think of it, is that why you said the Korean brother and I share the same shoes? Did you say that because he and I are greatly affected by our parental orientation and from time to time find ourselves in conflict with biblical instructions?"

"You got it! The details are different, but the principle is the same. There is a tension between parental influence and divine instructions."

"As far as possessions are concerned, I'll admit that there are times when my attitude changes for the better because I have certain material possessions. For example, on payday I am flying high, but when my money is low, I tend to worry. I get a sense of security from material possessions. Wow! I share the same struggles with each of the people I encountered."

"That is right. Every human does. When we don't know who we really are, we can easily become something that we are not. When we base our identity on anything other than Dad, we make three terrible errors.

"The first error we make is that we diminish our true value. As a member of the human race, every person alive is precious in the sight of Dad. It doesn't matter where they live or what language they speak. Their cultural heritages don't matter. They are all precious to Dad. He has an overwhelming love for every one of them."

"Are you telling me that God loves those who do wrong and those who do right the same?"

"I am glad you asked that question, but let me ask you a question in response. Have you ever done anything wrong?"

"Uh...yeah, I guess you can say that."

"Did Dad love you when you were doing wrong?"

"I guess He did."

"Well, I guess you answered your own question. Dad's love is not based on whether you do right or wrong. His love is based on two factors. First it is based on who we are. We are His children. We are the only creatures who are created in His image and in His likeness. Since we are His offspring He is obligated to love us. Let me put it this way. Do you love your children based on how good or bad they are, or do you love them because they are your children?"

"I love them because they are my children."

"Exactly. You may not like their behavior, but they are still your children. Because of their misbehavior, they may not enjoy all of the wonderful things that come along with being your children, but you still love them. Dad is the same way. He doesn't wait until we begin to behave a certain way before He begins to love us. In fact, whenever we misbehave, Dad uses His love as a means to transform us. I'll tell you more about His transforming love a little later, but for now I want to share the second reason why He loves you.

"His love is based on who He is. Dad is love, and therefore He is obligated by His own nature to love. He can't get around it. He can't deny it. He has to love at all times. Everything about Him has to pass through His love. His justice has to pass through His love. His judgment has to pass through His love. His mercy has to pass through His love. Even His anger has to pass through His love. You may not always love Him, but He always loves you unconditionally.

"Dad wants a love relationship with you so you can fully enjoy all of the blessings that come with being a part of His family. He wants the best for everyone at all times and under every situation. He wants all of His children to live long and prosperous lives. Everything He does, He does with these factors in mind. I want to be absolutely clear here: Dad loving unconditionally does not mean that He has no standards. Nor does it mean He will not judge or discipline you. In fact, He will judge and discipline you rightly because of His love.

"Now can we get back to the errors we make when we base our identity on anything other than Dad?"

"Yes, you have answered my question," I replied.

"The second error we make is denying Dad the intimacy He desires to have with us. Dad desires to be the central focus of our lives. He wants to be emotionally and mentally connected to us. He wants us to love Him with our entire being. When we base our identity on anything else, essentially we are denying Him what he desires most—to be our Dad."

"I had no idea that God was that interested in my life. I mean, I knew that he loved me, but I had no idea to what extent. I am totally blown away by what you are sharing with me."

"Frankly, this is only the tip of the iceberg."

"There is more?"

"A whole lot more!"

"Whoa!"

"Here is the third error we make when we base our identity on something other than Dad. We fail to appreciate the value of others. We live in a world that is divided by classism, racism, sexism, nationalism, heightism, weightism, neighborhoodism, religionism. The rich think they are better than the poor. One race thinks they are superior to another. Males think they are smarter than females. One nation thinks it's more powerful than another. One group tries to diminish the significance of the other so that they can justify mistreatment. All of these antagonistic divisions have come about as a result of our failure to recognize our true identity. When we fail to recognize that we are all created in the image of a wonderful and mighty Dad, we fight against one another instead of fighting for one another."

"Likeness, in light of everything you have shared with me, I can clearly see the error of our ways, but how do we get to where God wants us to be?"

"I thought you would never ask! For me to answer your question, we are going to have to go back before we can go forward."

"What do you mean by 'go back before we go forward'?"

"I am going to have to take you back to the beginning—back to Dad's original plan for His children. Life as you know it is not as it was intended. It is my pleasure to share His magnificent plan with you because Dad's plan for his children is truly amazing!"

Chapter 4

Dad's Magnificent Plan

Likeness stopped pacing back and forth. He paused for a second directly in front of me with his hands folded in front of him. As he began to talk again, he started backing up toward the canvas behind him.

"As a child of Dad, you have absolutely no idea how awesome you are! I want you to know that when Dad decided to create you, He put all of His God-ness into the work of your creation. He spared none of His creative genius in His desire to have you as His child. His predominant thought was to have a loving relationship with someone who would be birthed out of Him, someone who would represent him, someone who would rule like him, someone who would be in His image and likeness. Dad wanted a child to call His very own! In order to fulfill His most precious desire, Dad took several unprecedented actions."

Likeness stopped directly in front of the canvas behind him, then took one more step backward and disappeared into the canvas. I could no longer see him, but I could hear him. The canvas was instantly converted into what I would describe as a three-dimensional movie screen. However, I quickly learned that it was more than just a movie screen. In an instant, Likeness, the canvas, and I became one. Likeness became a voice in my head, and the screen became my vision. Each of us had our own responsibilities. Likeness was the voice narrating everything that took place; the canvas became the physical manifestation of everything Likeness spoke; and I was there as an inquisitive observer. Frankly, I was amazed and confused at the same time. I was amazed because it happened so fast and confused because I didn't know how it had happened, but I decided to trust in what was happening. By now I knew Likeness was unpredictable, so I readied myself for what I would learn.

Meanwhile Likeness continued to talk as if everything were normal. His words came to life with corresponding illustrations. As he spoke, I saw key elements of what he said in breathtaking detail. I felt like a little child taking part in a Disney production. It was utterly amazing!

Likeness said, "The first unprecedented action He took was to create the heavens and the earth."

Immediately, as far as my eyes could see, an infinite number of galaxies, planets, moons, and stars spread out like diamonds against the pitch-black darkness of space. It was as if I were suspended in space standing right beside Dad as He created this celestial masterpiece. It was so real to me that I felt as if I could reach out and touch each one.

Likeness continued, "Out of this vast array of galaxies, Dad chose one galaxy. Out of the one galaxy, He chose one planet. Out of the one planet, He selected one place. Out of the one place, He selected one creature to call His own. Out of sheer nothingness Dad began to create what no one else knew could exist. Out of the vastness of His imagination, He thought of some of the most marvelous creations ever seen. All of the heavenly host were amazed.

Once Dad selected one planet, He busied Himself with the work of making a home for the children He desired. For six days He created one masterpiece after another: light and darkness; heaven and earth; dry land and seas; mountains and valleys; plants, flowers, fruits, and vegetables; the sun, moon, and stars; birds of the air and fish of the sea; creeping things and crawling things. He prepared a breathtaking paradise."

With every word Likeness spoke, a magnificent scene unfolded. The first thing I noticed was a warm and gentle breeze. The air had a freshness I have never experienced before, and it gave me a feeling of exuberance I had never known. Then I saw darkness turn to light. And oh, what light! It was brighter and more brilliant than I have ever seen. In fact, the brightness caused me to shield my face at first, but somehow my eyes adjusted quickly so that I could enjoy everything that followed. I could not tell what the source of the light was, but instinctively I knew it represented the presence of God.

It was truly a marvel to behold, but things were happening so fast that I didn't have time to linger on any one thing. I saw the brilliance of the sun and felt the warm embrace of its heat. I saw the majesty of a full moon against the boldness of a blue sky. I saw water burst forth from the depths of the earth in waves and waves of splendor. I saw land appear, dividing oceans and rivers and streams. I saw the elevation of mountains and the perfect balance of valleys. I saw trees of every kind spring forth and begin to populate the earth. I saw plants and flowers of all colors, shapes, and sizes pushing their way out of the earth as if they were on assignment to beautify the planet. Then all of a sudden, as though it were a natural progression, the smell of the plants and flowers saturated the air with a delightfully intoxicating fragrance.

As if that weren't enough to convince me of Dad's magnificent plan, fruits and vegetables began to join in the chorus of creation. I saw the birth and maturation of every kind of fruit imaginable. It was as if time were put on fast forward. I saw all kinds of apple trees, orange trees, grapefruit trees, pear trees, avocado trees, mango trees, and banana trees. I saw watermelon, kiwi, dates, figs, and more. The vegetables would not be outdone as they added to the splendor of this magnificent scene. Lush green broccoli crowns stretched out toward the sun; ripe, plump, red tomatoes danced upon their vines; yellow and green squash spread themselves liberally along the ground; Brussels sprouts clung together like tiny cabbages; and golden stalks of corn waved their bushy green heads in rhythm with the breeze. There was vegetation as far as my eyes could see.

Then the parade of wildlife began. I saw flocks and flocks of birds of all kinds. There were blue jays, robins, parrots, sparrows, ducks, geese, hummingbirds, swans, pelicans, and several birds I could not name. There were big birds, small birds, and birds in between. There were red ones, yellow ones, white ones, black ones, gold ones, spotted ones, striped ones, and birds of many colors. They whistled, they chirped, they squawked, they honked, and they cooed. Their sound seemed to fill the sky with excitement and adulation for their Creator.

Then came a rumble that seemed to shake the whole earth. Herds and herds of animals began to flood the landscape. Elephants, giraffes, lions, bears, sheep, oxen, monkeys, wolves, anteaters, porcupines, skunks, and a host of other wildlife became a part of Dad's unfolding plan.

Then I heard Likeness say, "Now that you have a glimpse of Dad's overall creation, let me show you where your birth takes place."

"Don't you mean the birth of mankind?" I shouted, as if Likeness could not hear me because I couldn't see him.

"No need to shout. I am right here with you. I have simply taken on another form."

"But why did you do that? It seems so strange."

"It is not important that you see me. It is only important that you see Dad. I am only a messenger, and I never want to get in the way of what Dad wants to teach you. Now to answer your first question, no, I do not mean the birth of mankind. I mean your birth. In Dad's family we are all connected. There is no 'them' or 'they.' There is only 'we' and 'us.' What you call the birth of mankind is really your birth because man's identity has never really changed. In Dad's mind we are all the same—we are His children."

"Oh, I see."

And with that, Likeness, took me to a barren landscape. There was just rich black dirt as far as the eye could see. The bareness of the land took me by surprise after seeing and hearing all of the wonderful sights and sounds of creation. The only thing about the land that showed any promise was a huge river that ran through it and divided into four smaller rivers.

"Where are we, and why are we here?" I asked

"This is the place of your birth."

"But it's barren. There are no birds, no fruit, no vegetation, no trees, no plants, no flowers, and no animals. There is no fragrance. There is no beauty. Compared to what I have already seen, this place looks terrible! Who would want to pick a place like this after all of the magnificent things we just experienced? I don't understand. Why would..."

Likeness cut me off before I could finish my last thought. "I'll tell you who: Dad! That's who!"

His response hit me like a bolt of lightning. I had opened my big mouth a bit too early. At that point I felt it might be best for me to listen, so I remained silent.

"This is the place of Dad's next unprecedented actions. Up to this point in creation, none of the heavenly host had ever seen Dad use His hands. Everything He wanted to accomplish, He spoke into existence. Dad's words alone have all the power they need to accomplish whatever He wants. Dad used His words as tools of creation. He had no need to use His hands. But in the case of Dad's next two actions He decided to actually use His hands. These were two of the most profound acts any of us had ever seen. He formed you out of the dust of the earth, and He planted a garden for you with His very own hands.

"When Dad decided to make you out of the dust of the earth, He took something that was virtually worthless and turned it into something of the highest earthly value. Then to make your creation even more extraordinary, Dad shared His very essence with you by breathing into you the sustaining force of life! With one breath, you became a vibrant spiritual being created in Dad's image.

Image signifies form. It's not your physical form that causes you to resemble Dad; it is your spiritual form. Dad made you a spiritual being with an earthly body! Your creation ushered in the first covenant between divinity and humanity! Unlike all of the other earthly creatures, you were endowed with eternal life and carried in your body Dad's fundamental nature. Not only were you created in Dad's image, but you were also created in His likeness. Likeness signifies function. You were created not just to look like Dad but also to act like Dad. We will talk more about your likeness a little later on, but for now I want to talk about Dad planting a garden.

Dad hand-picked this specific place to do a special work. As you have observed, nothing appeared to be special about the place that Dad chose. The outward appearance may not have been attractive, but there certainly was something special on the inside. Dad knew that the place He chose would produce a garden of paradise. So He planted a garden there. He laid aside His royal crown and lowered Himself to the position of a gardener. He wanted this place to be special, so He had hands-on involvement. He thoroughly enjoyed every minute He spent preparing this place for you. Like a parent, He busied Himself with the task of preparing a place for His firstborn.

The heavenly host was aghast at the notion that the King of Kings and Lord of Lords wanted to do such a thing himself. We would have gladly carried out this task on His behalf. We were completely befuddled, but as we watched Him carry out this act of love, we understood why He had to do it Himself. This creation required the type of love that only Dad could give. It was important for Him to put His head, heart, and hands into this work."

"Wow! After hearing your explanation, this barren land looks pretty good."

"Let me show you just how beautiful it is."

Once again brilliant light exploded on the scene, accompanied by the warmth of a gentle breeze. The barren land quickly began to disappear. Radical transformation began to take place. Every inch of barren land began to be covered with lush green leaves, colorful flowers, and an assortment of plants and trees of all kind. The agricultural growth spread like wildfire across the barren landscape. Fruit popped up everywhere. The plant life was so abundant that I could smell the mingled scent of vegetables, fruit, and flowers throughout the entire garden.

Everything was immaculate! There were no blemishes at all on any of the fruit, vegetables, or flowers. The open fields were a deep rich green without any variance. I was fascinated by grapes the size of grapefruits hanging heavy on their vines. Slowly but surely, the barren land began to take on the personality of paradise. Compared to everything else I saw, this place was the most beautiful of all. I remember thinking, "This is a place fit for a king."

At that very moment I was struck with amazement! My gaze landed upon something that completely took my breath away! In the middle of the garden was a tree that was different from all other trees. The trunk was wide and massive. From the height of the tree, I could tell that its roots ran deep into the ground. The bark was a rustic bronze color which looked like gold wrapping around the tree as it glistened in the afternoon sun. The strong, sturdy branches hung very low and appeared to be bursting with life. The huge leaves were the deepest green I had ever seen. Each one was wider and longer than the size of a man's head. The leaves were so well defined that I could see thick veins running through each one. The combination of the branches and leaves created soothing shade from the heat of the summer sun. At the end of each branch was something I found hard to comprehend. There were clusters of fruit and in each cluster there was a variety of twelve different fruits. I could not identify any of the fruits, but I could tell that they too were bursting with life.

I was so mesmerized by this tree that I completely forgot about Likeness. As I admired the fruit, I heard Likeness say, "It's magnificent, isn't it?"

His voice startled me. "Yes, it is!" I replied. "It is beyond magnificent! It is incredible!"

"This is the tree of life. It is another of Dad's special gifts to His children. It is a tree like no other. It bears fresh fruit monthly, and its leaves are used for healing."

"Wow! I have never seen a tree with a variety of fruit before. How is this possible?"

"There are two things I want you to always remember and never forget. The first is that nothing is impossible for Dad. The second is that there are some things Dad does that we will never understand. If you and I could explain everything there is to know about Dad, that would make you and I Dad's dad. All we need to know is that Dad knows what He is doing."

As Likeness answered my question, my eyes landed on another tree that I hadn't noticed before. Like the tree of life, this tree was located in the center of the garden. It was just as impressive. In fact, at first glance it looked just like the tree of life. It was the same height; the bark was the same rustic color; the leaves were almost the same shape and size; and the branches hung low. Upon closer examination, however, I saw that it was different. This tree had two different types of fruit. The fruit looked delightful and appealing. In fact, it was so alluring that I found myself drawn to touch it. Just as I was about to touch the fruit, I heard Likeness say, "Don't touch it. I know it looks inviting, but outward appearances can fool you. Not everything that looks good is good. This is the tree of the knowledge of good and evil. It is the tree that began your downward spiral."

"So is this tree poisonous?"

"No, the tree is not poisonous. The tree is forbidden. We will talk more about this tree in just a few minutes, but for now I want to continue to share with you a few other unprecedented actions that Dad took for you."

I said, "This garden is truly amazing! I can't believe Dad sent you to show all of this to me. I can't believe my eyes. It is all so beautiful. I feel like I am having a wonderful dream, and I am hoping that I never wake up! Just these two trees alone are more magnificent than anything else I have ever seen."

I was so overwhelmed with emotions that tears began to run down my cheeks.

Likeness responded, "I know how you feel—especially when you consider that He did all of this for you! As I stated earlier, Dad spared none of His creative genius when it came to preparing a place for you."

I was speechless.

As I continued to admire the two trees standing side by side, Likeness continued, "There are two more unprecedented acts Dad did that I want to share with you."

"To be honest, I don't know if I can take any more."

"I know what you mean. Dad's love is overwhelming once you begin to fully understand it. But I must complete my assignment, so we must go on."

"Okay—let's do it."

"Dad completely blew us away by what He did next. He put you to sleep, withdrew a portion of your core, and built one of the most gorgeous creatures any of us had ever seen. The creature had features that were different from yours, but in essence the creature was the same. The creation came to be known as woman because she was taken out of man. She too was created in Dad's image and likeness. She too was to enjoy eternal life. When Dad finished his handiwork, He was well pleased with everything He had done."

"I can understand why! All of this is utterly amazing!"

"Yes, it is. I am glad that you have enjoyed it. Now let's go back to the classroom."

The next thing I knew, we were back in the classroom setting. I was seated at the marble countertop facing the mirror. Certainly I was startled by the sudden change, but I quickly decided to ignore it. For a few seconds all I could see was the black canvas on the other side of the mirror. Then Likeness stepped out of the canvas and continued our conversation.

"The last unprecedented action that Dad took was to give you complete and total rulership and dominion over all the earth. This phenomenal action essentially transferred rulership of the earth from Dad to His children. This meant that when Dad wanted to influence the operation of earth, He would normally operate through His children. At that very moment Dad gave us the ultimate gift: He gave us His vote of confidence. He put His trust and hopes in His children to govern the earth as He would. He did all of these magnificent acts for you so that you could create heaven right here on earth."

41

"This experience has definitely given me a whole new perspective on the creation story."

"I totally understand. Seeing events firsthand is always different from reading accounts of those same events. I wanted you to feel the experience."

"Well, you certainly accomplished your objective."

"That's good to hear!"

"But Likeness, I have a question. "

"What's that?"

"When I consider everything you have shown me thus far, what would make us give up all of what we had? That's the part that doesn't make any sense. We had everything anyone would ever want. We had a beautiful place to live, all the food and provisions we would ever need, power and authority, a wonderful Dad to guide us, and each other. What more could a person what? What went wrong?"

"That is a great question," said Likeness. "I guess it is time for me to introduce you to backward living."

"Backward living? What is backward living, and what does it have to do with the question I asked?"

"You'll see."

"Oh boy, here we go again!"

Chapter 5

Backward Living

Likeness began by asking, "How are your drawing skills? For this next learning experience you are going to have to draw a few diagrams. They are simple, but their implications are important for you to understand."

"Okay. I can do that. I have average drawing skills, so a diagram shouldn't be a problem."

"Great! Open your notebook to the first available page. At the top of your paper, I want you to write *Order of Dad*. Directly under the words, I want you to draw three separate ovals—one oval directly under the other."

I picked up the pen next to the notebook and did as Likeness requested.

"In the first oval I want you to write *spirit*. In the second I want you to write *soul*, and in the last I want you to write *body*."

I did so.

"Finally, I want you to draw an arrow above each oval, pointing upward.

I did so.

"What you are looking at is Dad's original design for your life."

I looked up from my paper and asked, "So Dad wanted us to be ovals and arrows?"

Likeness laughed and said, "Very funny, very funny," After he regained his composure, he continued, "The diagram in front of you represents Dad's original intent for your life. When you look at the diagram, you see the word *spirit* in the first oval, *soul* in the second oval, and *body* in the third. Now let me explain. Dad has given you a spirit so that you can be aware of and in constant contact with Him. Dad is a spirit; therefore, we must communicate with Him through spiritual means. Through your spirit, Dad gives you insight, inspiration, and intuition.

"Now let's talk about the second oval marked *soul*. Your soul enables you to think, feel, and act. Dad gave you a soul so that you can be aware of and in constant contact with what is going on inside of you. In addition, your soul enables you to relate to others. Your soul has been given the freedom of choice. It is the command center of your life. I call it the head, heart, and hand center because it negotiates between your divinity and your humanity.

"The last oval is marked *body*. Dad gave you a body so you can be aware of and in constant contact with the world around you. Your body has five senses that enable you to see, smell, hear, touch, and taste. The body represents the carnal nature of man. Without a body, you would have no physical presence in this world.

"Dad's intention for you is to function in the order arranged on your diagram. His original plan was for you to be in a spiritual relationship with Him. He has always wanted to be the primary influence in your life. From that relationship, His spiritual influence would affect the condition of your soul, and the condition of your soul would influence the behavior of your body.

"As I told you earlier, you are a spiritual being created in Dad's image and likeness. Because you are a spiritual being, you will always be in Dad's image, but your functionality determines if you will operate in His likeness. Looking like Him doesn't automatically mean you will act like Him."

Likeness continued. "It is writing time again. I want you to write this down in big, bold letters and underline it. Are you ready?"

"Any time you are."

"Write *Order of Evil* at the top of a clean sheet of paper. Look at the words and tell me what you see."

"I see the word *evil*. I see a word that has destroyed the lives of many people. I see a word that promotes hate and division. I see a word that can never promote love. I see a word that corrupts the imagination of men and women. I see a word that is in direct conflict with everything God stands for."

"Very good. I see you have some really strong feelings about this word. I can't say I blame you. But there is one thing I want you to see that you haven't mentioned. *Evil* is the word *live* spelled backward."

"Wow—I have never seen that!"

"I understand. Don't feel bad. Sometimes we tend to overlook the obvious. Here is my point. Evil always tries to get us to live our lives backward. Are you ready to draw another diagram?"

"Yes."

"Okay. Under the words *Order of Evil,* draw three separate ovals, one under the other vertically, just like you did in the other diagram. In the first oval write the word *body.* In the next oval write the word *soul.* In the last oval write the word *spirit.*"

Once again I did as Likeness requested.

"Now draw arrows pointing downward from the bottom of each oval. What you have is a diagram of Evil's desire."

Order of Evil

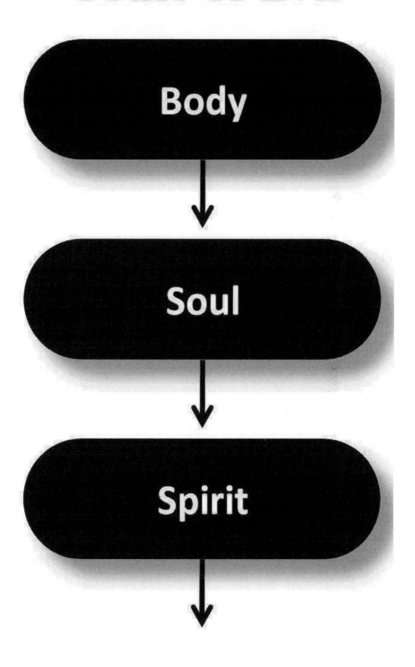

"Evil wants us to live our lives based on the dictates of our carnal nature (body). Evil constantly tries to get us to live from the outside in instead of the inside out. In other words, Evil attempts to get us to pay more attention to the world around us than the world within us. Instead of our spiritual relationship with Dad being our primary influence, Evil tries to manipulate our carnal nature and become our primary influence. As you can see by the diagram, if Evil is able to convince you of its *backward living* model, then it influences the condition of the soul (how you think, act, and feel), and it weakens, suppresses, and eventually destroys your spiritual connection with Dad. In the end, you wind up being completely blind to who you really are. You are cut off from your source of strength—your spiritual connection to Dad—and you are led away into a life of pitiful outcomes. If you find yourself ensnared by this backward way of living and you are guilty of the wrong you have chosen to do, you are more readily willing to identify yourself by what you have done wrong than by who Dad has made you to be. This Evil model causes you to completely lose touch with your true identity."

"Like the people we met on the city streets?"

"Exactly like the people we met on the city streets. The influence of Evil in their lives was not readily apparent, but when we looked beneath the surface, we could see that they were all convinced by Evil that their identity rested in superficial associations. Evil knows it can never do anything to truly destroy your image, so it attacks your likeness and uses your wrongdoing as a means to convince you that you aren't who you should be.

"What you don't know is that Evil has no power in and of itself. It can only have the power you choose to give it. Since you're the one who has been given dominion over the earth, you can choose to deny Evil its power or give it power through the choices you make."

"Where did Evil come from?"

"Evil originated in an angelic being that was created by Dad. This angelic being abused his freedom by trying to become greater than Dad. As a result of his rebellion, he was dismissed from his heavenly home and became a disembodied spirit. Since he was originally created by Dad, he cannot totally shake his dependence on Him. However, because of the evil in his heart, he is in self-willed opposition to Dad. His goal is to convince as many as he can to rebel against Dad and therefore share in his misery. This evil disembodied spirit understands the Law of Manifestation. He uses that law to his advantage to affect the thoughts, emotions, and actions of mankind, thereby manifesting evil into the world."

"What is the Law of Manifestation?"

"The Law of Manifestation is the law of how everything comes into being. Write down this acronym: S.T. E. A. M. The "S" stands for Spirit, the "T" for Thought, the "E" for Emotions, the "A" for Action, and the "M" for Manifestation. This acronym represents the process through which thoughts become things.

Now let me explain. Everything begins in the spiritual realm. I guess the simplest way for you to understand this truth is to remember that Dad is the Spirit who created the heavens and the earth. Before the world came into existence in the physical realm, it existed in the spiritual realm. So we can conclude that everything happens in the spirit before it manifests in the physical. It has always been that way, and it will always be that way. Somewhere deep within the heart of every man and woman, they know this is true. No matter how much they try to intellectualize what they think about the existence of the spiritual world, intuitively everyone knows the spiritual world exists.

"Now let's move on to the subject of thought. There is a spirit behind every thought—a spirit of Dad or a spirit of Evil. A spirit is of Dad or Evil based on one thing: Does it communicate love, or does it communicate hate? If it is love, the spirit is of Dad. If it is hate, the spirit is of Evil.

"Your thoughts affect your emotions. It is impossible to have happy thoughts and unhappy feelings. It is just as impossible to have happy feelings and unhappy thoughts. Your thoughts and emotions are inextricably interwoven. Your thoughts and emotions affect your actions. When the head and heart are in agreement, the hands usually follow suit.

"So now you understand that actions are influenced by emotions, emotions are influenced by thoughts, and thoughts are influenced by spirit.

"Finally, manifestation is the end result of it all. What started out spiritual ends up becoming material. Another way to think about it is this: The spirit is the seed. Thoughts are the root system which grows from the seed. Emotions are the stem, which grows out of the root system. Actions are the branches. And manifestation is the fruit. Through the Law of Manifestation, that which is unseen becomes seen. In other words, thoughts become things. This is what I call 'tracing the fruit to the root.' Evil understands this process all too well, and because many people are unaware that this law exists, they are manipulated into becoming agents of Evil."

"Why are we so inclined to fall into the temptations of Evil?"

"The spirit of Evil is crafty. Since Evil knows its own limitations, it preys on our Dad-given natural desires. He takes what we are inclined to naturally do and attempts to pervert it. For example, all of us have the desire to be loved. So what Evil will do is devise a strategy to underhandedly attack that desire. He will use any number of strategies—promiscuity, homosexuality, child abuse, adultery, etc. Evil's goal is to do anything that will cause us to deviate from Dad's original design.

"Ultimately Evil wants to be so deeply embedded into our thinking that what is perverted seems natural and what is natural seems perverted. For example, sexual promiscuity has become common behavior for most of society. It is so common that those who choose not to indulge in it are labeled in a negative way. You can tell when Evil has truly captured a person's life: They walk around in darkness and think that they are in the light! In other words, they are ignorant of the detrimental nature of their lives because they are unfamiliar with Dad's plan. Have I answered your question?"

"Yes, you have. In fact you have gone beyond answering my question. I can see evidence in my everyday life of some of the things you have mentioned, especially when it comes to how evil perverts my natural desires. I have fallen prey to Evil's manipulation of my natural desires several times. I have certainly lived backward during my lifetime."

"Everyone has. No one on earth is exempt."

"Yeah, but how do we overcome the influence of Evil in our lives so that we can become what God intended for us?"

"You simply accept Dad's plan to be reunited with Him."

"Are you talking about Dad's plan for reconciliation?"

"Yeah. That's what you call it, but to Dad it's a family reunion."

Chapter 6

A FAMILY REUNION AND A SURPRISED GUEST

Likeness was back to his pacing. Once again his hands were folded behind his back and his head was held high. He reminded me of a philosopher because he always gazed upward. He began, "Do you remember the tree I told you not to touch when we were in the garden?"

"Yes, I do. It had such an alluring attraction."

"Well, as I stated earlier that was the tree of the knowledge of good and evil. It was the tree that led to the downward spiral of your family."

"What is so bad about the tree?"

"It is the tree of the knowledge of good and evil."

"I don't understand. What is so bad about that?"

"Let me explain. This tree was forbidden because Dad understood that the Evil One will come at you in two ways. Either he will come at you with something evil, or he will come at you with something good. Once they have experienced evil with all of its alluring deception, many people are not likely to ever try it again. So instead of approaching you with the same evil, he will approach you with something that looks good. Remember, he is a deceiver, and his greatest deception comes from offering something good in place of something that comes from Dad. In your words, he will use good to distract you from God!

"Let me be even clearer. The Evil One will use any means necessary to derail you from your Dad-given destiny. For those who are immature in their relationship with Dad, he will use evil because their immaturity blinds them from its harmful effects. But for those who are mature, he will use good because chances are his evil schemes have already been exposed and they know better than to trust Evil again. Either way the objective is the same: destroy your likeness to Dad!"

"Okay, Likeness, I get it, but why did God put the tree in the garden in the first place? I mean, if He didn't want us to touch it, why put it there?"

"Dad put the tree there because He understands that true love offers choices. There is no other way to determine real love. If you didn't have any choices, how would you know what your real preferences were? You wouldn't. If you didn't have any choices, how would you know whom you really loved? You wouldn't. Love is about making choices.

"Dad gave you clear instructions concerning the tree. The only thing that determined your love for Him was the option you chose. Dad didn't make you a robot. He made you a man with choices. In the beginning He gave you the choice to listen to Him or to pick another way. You were tempted with something that appeared to be good, and you made the wrong choice. Your choices allow the Evil One to take up residence in your head and heart and drag you further and further away from Dad. The problem was never the tree; the problem was the response to instructions associated with the tree. Dad gave clear instructions concerning it. He said it was off limits. The real problem was disobedience."

"So how did disobedience affect the relationship between God and me?"

"It didn't. It only affected the companionship."

"I don't understand. What do you mean that it affected the companionship and not the relationship? What is the difference?"

"Companionship has to do with interacting with one another; relationship has to do with being related to one another. Like any great parent, He shared the consequences of what would happen if you decided not to follow His instructions. He told you that you would no longer enjoy the gift of eternal life. Your only inheritance would be death and damnation.

"The gravity of the consequences Dad shared let you know two things: Dad was serious about His instructions, and He loved you enough to discipline you. Although these consequences were severe, He would never disown you. In other words, you would always be in relationship with Him, but your companionship would be lost. Let me explain it this way: When your children misbehave, does their misbehavior change the relationship or the companionship? Are you still their father? Are they still your children?"

"Well, when you put it that way, I would have to say it changes the companionship because I will never disown them as my children!"

"That's right. You may discipline them, which temporarily changes the companionship, but the relationship is still intact. You are still their father and they are still your children regardless of what they do. With Dad it is no different. He will always be Dad whether you recognize Him as Dad or not. Your misbehavior may warrant discipline and therefore affect the companionship, but the relationship remains unaffected."

"That makes perfect sense to me."

"Good, because there is more. Since Dad was and is and will always be such a loving Father, He pursued you in an attempt to renew your companionship with Him. Dad established family values, better known as commandments, as a roadmap to get you back on track. Unfortunately, because of the corruption in you caused by Evil, you were unable to live up to His expectations. Instead of getting you back on track, Dad's family values only magnified your wrongdoings. From one generation to another, you violated each one of Dad's family values. Instead of developing the companionship He desired with you, your choices moved you further and further away. Your attraction toward evil quickly became a permanent stumbling block between you and Dad."

"How has evil become a permanent stumbling block to me?"

"I'll answer that question by sharing this exercise with you. A few of Dad's family values include the following: He tells you that you shouldn't lie, you shouldn't steal, and you shouldn't lust after anyone or anything. Now let me ask you a few questions, and you provide me with honest answers. I must warn you that my line of questioning is going to be a little uncomfortable, but bear with me. You will better understand as we complete this exercise. Okay?"

"Sure, go right ahead,"

"Have you ever stolen anything?"

"Yeah, I guess so."

"What does that make you?"

"I guess that makes me a thief. But it was only something small like a dollar."

"Does it matter if it was a dollar or one million dollars?"

"I guess not."

"You are right. It doesn't matter; you are still a thief. Have you ever lied?"

"I...uh...may have told a small lie or two in my life."

"The size of the lie doesn't matter. Does it make a difference whether you told a big lie or a small lie? What would you call a person who told a lie, regardless of the size?"

"I guess I would call him a liar."

"Correct again."

"Have you ever lusted after another?"

"I...I...have to say yes...but that was a long time ago."

"What does that make you?"

"Someone who has lust in my heart."

By the time Likeness asked me the third question, I began to feel really convicted. Until he asked me these questions, I didn't realized how many of Dad's family values I had disobeyed. No one had ever presented the Ten Commandments like this before. I began to think about some of the other commandments. I asked myself if I loved Dad more than I loved everything else. Because I couldn't answer with a resounding yes, I had to conclude that I didn't. I was about to go further into thought when I heard Likeness speak.

"Okay, so let's summarize. By your own admission you have lied, stolen, and lusted. You do realize that we have only covered three of the ten family values and you have violated all three, don't you? Why do you think your answers were all yeses? Do you think it is because you are a bad person? Or could it be that the presence of evil has become a permanent stumbling block in your life?"

"I see what you mean. I have been lulled to sleep by the presence of Evil."

"On the surface that is true. Everyone has been tempted by evil, but remember the choice was yours to make. Dad gave you the ability to choose. You can't blame Evil for the bad decisions you made. Dad is justified in judging you according to the choices you have made. Looking at your choices, do you think you deserve a reward or punishment?"

"If my punishment or reward is based on the three questions you asked, honestly, I would have to say punishment."

"What if punishment meant that you would have to permanently dwell in a place set aside for those who choose evil?"

"I hate to admit it, but Dad would be right to send me there."

"You are right. Dad would be justified to send you there."

"Likeness, I need to ask you a question."

"Go right ahead."

"Does Dad reward or punish us based solely on our ability to live up to His family values? If He does, none of us would ever be rewarded."

"You are right. None of you would be rewarded. Everyone has violated Dad's family values. But here is where the family reunion begins. Let me explain. When I asked you those three questions, I did so knowing that you would answer yes to each one. There is not a man or woman alive who could honestly answer no to any of the questions I asked you. All of mankind has violated Dad's family values. All of mankind has been influenced by Evil. All of mankind deserves to be severely punished. All of mankind has broken Dad's heart—not just once, not just twice, but countless times. None of mankind has lived life as they should.

"When Dad recognized that His family values were disregarded and that all of His children had gone astray, He did something that seemed to make no sense at all. He did what He did only because of His love. By all indications, it made sense for Him to give up on mankind. You had become something other than He intended. You had turned your affections toward other interests. The behavior of mankind had gotten so bad that you had become His adversaries. You disregarded all of the wonderful plans He had for you. Mankind had completely turned your back on Him.

"Despite all of these things, Dad's love would not be denied. He didn't choose to love you because you were so lovable; He chose to love you because He is so loving. His fatherly love would not allow Him to give up on you. His love was a choice He made all on His own. Instead of condemning you by giving you what you rightly deserved, He decided to redeem you by giving you something you didn't deserve. Instead of punishing you, He implemented a plan to transform you.

"Once again Dad was about to do something unprecedented. For the second time, He decided that He would leave His heavenly home with all of its splendor and majesty. This time He would clothe Himself in the same flesh that He created with His own hands. He decided to come to your rescue himself. Not as your Dad—the one who created you, but as your Older Brother—the one who had compassion for you. He decided to take on another form—not as God but as one of His own children. He didn't come as a father figure to scold you for your wrongdoing. He came as a brother, subjecting Himself to the same trials and challenges you face. He came to understand you, not to condemn you. He came to redeem you from your inevitable end.

"Dad's plan for a family reunion was ingenious. Since He knew that mankind was incapable of fulfilling His family values and that the consequences of failure would have to be judged according to His moral excellence, He came to fulfill His standards in your place, so that He could exchange His obedience for your disobedience and thereby reconcile you back into good standing with Himself. He removed the penalty that your evil deeds deserved by paying the cost for all of your wrongdoings through the sacrificial life of your Older Brother.

"Dad is just. He has to judge rightly. His love will not allow Him to do otherwise. His love obligates Him to punish where punishment is required and to discipline where discipline is required. Therefore someone had to pay the penalty for your disobedience. He decided that He would be the one to pay! So He sacrificed Himself so that you might go free. Your Older Brother satisfied the requirements of the family values by paying the price for you with His life. All you have to do is openly receive the love that Dad offered you through the sacrifice of your Older Brother. When you do so, your reward is assured—not based on your own goodness but on the goodness of your Dad who loved you enough to make the ultimate sacrifice!"

"So do we still have to live by Dad's family values even though our Older Brother has done so in our place?" I asked.

"Yes. But the motivation for doing so has changed. You don't live according to Dad's family values in order to get His approval. You do it because you already have His approval. The significance of Dad's family values doesn't change. They are just as important today as they were from the very beginning. Your response to His incredible love should be a willingness to live by His family values. Dad interprets love in one way—obedience to His family values."

"Likeness, really when I consider all of the wonderful provisions Dad has made for us, I guess being obedient to Dad is the least we can do."

"Yes. You are right once again. But there is more you need to understand about Dad's love. After your Older Brother had completed His assignment, Dad gave you yet another gift. He gave you a Spiritual companion—someone who would be a consistent reminder to you of who you are and who Dad is. This Spiritual companion is Dad in yet another form. Unlike your Older Brother, who came in a physical form, this time He would be an abiding presence—not *with* you but *in* you. His job is to restore you back to Dad's original plan for you. He is the great rejuvenator, restoring you into the likeness of Dad. He is yet another expression of Dad's gift of love to you.

"He enabled you to return to your proper place as the one who has dominion over the earth. This gift of love restored your power. You are no longer subject to Evil because of this gift. Evil has been conquered and has lost its ugly grip on you. This gift of love restored your privileges. Once again you are heirs of Dad's family. You are children with a divine destiny. Because of this abiding presence, you should always know, beyond a shadow of a doubt, that the purpose of your lives is to reflect His image and His likeness. He has taken you beyond the limitations of this mirror. You should no longer think of yourselves as only flesh and bones because your true identity is based on what has happened inside and not on what happens outside. The power of our Dad now lives in you!"

When Likeness finished speaking, I have to admit I was flabbergasted. It was hard for me to imagine being loved as much as Dad loved us. All I could think to say at the time was, "Is there any more to Dad's love?" After that question, Likeness was off to the races again.

"Yes, as a matter of fact there is. All of the information I have shared with you during our time together is rooted in Dad's love. The questions you had about Genesis 1:26–27 can only be answered to the extent that you understand Dad's love."

Likeness stopped pacing and walked toward me. The look on his face was warm and tender. He appeared to be smiling with his entire face. His eyebrows were lifted, and his lips were curled upward into a half smile. He kneeled down so that he and I were face to face and He said softly, "I am that abiding presence! I am He who is responsible to remind you of Daddy's love. I am the one who is your comforter. I am the one who strengthens you whenever you are weak. I am the one who reminds you of what Dad has said. I am the one who goes before you to plead your case to Him.

"Yes, you call me Likeness because right now when you look at me, I look like you. I came looking like you so that you would accept me. But my job is to transform you so that you become to Dad what I have become to you. When Dad looks in the mirror, He wants to see you—not just outwardly but inwardly as well. My job is to complete the work that Dad began in you. You already have His image; no one and nothing can ever take that away. My job is to transform you into His likeness. Although I am standing on the outside of you, I am the abiding presence that resides in you. When I spoke to you earlier about the three terrible errors we make whenever we base our identity on anything other than Dad, I said 'we' rather than 'you.' I did that because it is important for you to know that you and I are meant to be one. I have come to bring the best of you to you! Dad has given me permission to stand before you to assure you of His abiding presence within you. I am here to love you into greatness!"

With every word Likeness spoke, my heart simply melted. Here I was thinking that he was an angelic being who looked like me. I had no idea that He was the indwelling presence of God! I didn't know what to say or what to feel; my mind and emotions were completely captivated by what was happening. But I can tell you that I will never forget that moment as long as I live! That was the day when I talked to God face to face! The peace I felt at that moment was something I could never describe.

LIKENESS

And God said, "Let us make man...after in our likeness."
(Gen 1:26 NIV)
"Likeness represents function and can be changed!"

Chapter 7

DAD IS UNCOMMON LOVE!

Likeness backed away slightly and began to rise from His kneeling position. As soon as He stood up, I noticed that He looked different. He still resembled me, but He had a radiance that I had not noticed before. Quite frankly, after His shocking disclosure of who He was, I was completely in awe of the fact that He was standing in front of me. Although I heard what He said, it was still difficult for me to accept the fact that God cared for me so much that He came to me in the form of Likeness. The overwhelming nature of this whole experience changed how I viewed God. Likeness was right: God was my Dad, plain and simple. But I kept thinking to myself, "No one is going to believe this!"

Likeness said, "Yes, they will."

"Excuse me?" I retorted.

"You were thinking that no one is ever going to believe our encounter. Yes, they will. You are not the only person I have visited. Besides, what I have shown you so far is way too bizarre for you to make up on your own. It is a story worth believing."

"I don't know. To be honest, I am having a hard time believing it myself."

Likeness continued pacing. He didn't respond to my last statement, but said, "By now you understand that your image is as solid as steel.

It cannot be changed by anything or anyone. Regardless of who you thought you were, you have been and always will be Dad's child. The time has come for us to talk about your likeness to Dad. Your likeness refers to your functionality—how you think, feel, and act. As I stated earlier, just looking like Him doesn't mean you will act like Him."

"After everything you have shown me about Dad, I can't wait to learn what I need to do to act like Him. Whatever it will take, I am ready."

"That's great! I hope you feel that way after I explain to you what being like Dad really means. I sense that your heart is ready for the next part of our journey together."

"You bet! I am rip roaring to go!"

"Great! Then let's begin. When it comes to living your life in Dad's likeness, there is one thing you need to always remember and never forget. Dad is love! Now I know that on the surface that statement may sound trite because for several years mankind has overused the word *love*. As a consequence of overuse, it has been completely watered down and has lost most of its effectiveness and meaning."

"I agree. Everybody uses the word *love*, and it has become way too common."

"I am glad you agree. So then, you understand that it is important for me to clarify what I mean by 'Dad is love'?"

"Yes, I do."

"When I say 'Dad is love,' I am not saying that love is one of Dad's characteristics. I am saying that Dad *is* love. Love is Dad, and Dad is love. The two are inseparable. In other words, the kind of love I am referring to is the actual presence of Dad. Dad shows up in any and every true act of love. His presence is manifested whenever you share this kind of love. Because you have been created in His likeness, it is your responsibility to be the vessel through which Dad is shared with the rest of the world."

"What makes Dad's love so different from the love we experience in the world?"

"There are four characteristics of Dad's love that separate His love from the rest of the world. First, His love is *unusual*."

"Unusual?" That is a word I didn't expect you to use.

"I know, but I need to start here because you need to fully understand that Dad's love is far from common."

"I see."

"So as I just stated, His love is unusual. Here is what I mean. Worldly love is natural in scope and carnal in nature. It is based on one factor: feelings. If the relationship produces good feelings, then the love is strengthened. The moment that it fails to produce these feelings, the love is weakened. This kind of love is self-centered, self-serving, and self-satisfying. The lover is completely controlled by the loved one. In short, love is reduced to a feeling.

"Dad's love is unusual in the sense that it is not based on feeling. His love is a decision. It is a love of the will. His feelings are involved, but His feelings are secondary to His will. Think of it this way. He feels all the emotions you feel, but He doesn't allow his feelings to alter what He has ultimately decided to do. So He will cry when His heart is broken, just like you, but He will not allow His broken heart to dictate whether or not He will continue to love. He will stand by what He has decided, no matter what! This is what makes His love so unusual. His own feelings will never alter it!"

"Man, oh man! What you have just explained is unbelievable."

"We'll get to unbelievable in a minute, but for now let me give you the second reason Dad's love is different from worldly love. His love is *unlimited*. The extent of His love matches the intent of His love."

"I am almost too overwhelmed to ask, but what do you mean by 'the extent of His love matches the intent of His love'?"

"I'll explain it like this. Sometimes you can start out intending to love someone, but because of their prolonged imperfections, what you originally intended to do begins to wane in the face of their shortcomings. The magnitude of their problems far outweighs the measure of your love, and in the end what you intended to do is thwarted. At that point, the extent of your love fails to match the intent of your love. Somewhere along the line, your love runs out. You are unable to extend your love because it causes you too much pain. You become more concern about your emotional well-being than your love for the other person.

"With Dad this is not the case. His love never runs out. It never gives up. Our imperfections don't frustrate Him, and it doesn't matter how long it takes for our hearts to be changed. The extent of Dad's love matches the intent of His love. Since it was His intention from the beginning to love us, He remains committed to what He intended until His love accomplishes its goal. And of course its goal is to transform the heart of Dad's children and bring you back into a loving companionship with Him. When it comes to loving others, there is something that Dad fully understands. In order to be effective, love has to outlast anything that would try to deny its power.

"Another way of looking at Dad's love is this: If wrong is ever going to do right, then right has to remain right to convert that wrong, because if right ever decided to do wrong, then wrong would never have a model of what it means to do right. With this in mind, you can understand why it is imperative that Dad's love never fails. Its consistency transforms you and provides a model for you at the same time."

"Wow, Likeness. That was a mouthful," I said.

"I know. Dad's love is not only a mouthful, but sometimes it leaves you completely speechless! Dad's unlimited love has converted countless hearts. Just when you think that Dad has no more love to give, He relentlessly gives more until the loved one is totally captivated by His love. In our Family Book of Wisdom—the book you call the Bible—it is recorded that where wrongdoing thrives, Dad's grace (a product of Dad's love) abounds even more! Dad will never allow His love to be overcome by anything. He is love.

"The third characteristic of Dad's love which distinguishes it from other types of love is that it is *unconditional*. There is nothing you can do to earn it, and there is nothing you can do to lose it. It is not based on you at all."

"This is hard for me to understand because I thought that if we were obedient, Dad would love us more and if we were disobedient, Dad would love us less."

"If that were the case, Dad's love would be temporary and temperamental at best because there is never a time when you are always obedient. So His love would fluctuate based solely on how well you performed. In addition, Dad's love would be controlled by you instead of being controlled by Him. Many people think they can control Dad's love by their behavior, but nothing can be further from the truth. Dad's love does not waver or fluctuate based on human behavior. The unconditional nature of Dad's love allows His love to remain consistent."

"When I think about what you are saying, I understand. Although to be honest, I can't fully understand unconditional love. All of the love I have ever experienced seemed to have a long list of conditions attached to it. At the first sign of disappointment, the love is usually lost."

"I completely understand. That type of love is based solely on human ability. It is man's attempt to do on his own what only Dad can do through him. Without Dad's involvement, man's love will always fall short.

"The fourth characteristic of Dad's love is that it is *unbelievable.* To the human mind, Dad's love makes absolutely no sense at all."

"I am the first to agree with that statement, especially when I consider my own life. It is hard to believe that Dad could ever love me the way He does. I have done some things I am not proud of ,and I can't believe He loves me knowing everything I have done."

"That is exactly what makes Dad's love so unbelievable. Everyone else who loves you does so based on their limited knowledge of you. They don't know you as well as Dad does. In fact, they only know the portion of you that you are willing to share with them. Everything else is hidden from view. But with Dad, that is never the case. He knows everything there is to know about you. He knows every thought, every idea, every act, and every secret. Nothing is hidden from Him. You would think that with everything He knows, He would hesitate to care so much about you. But He doesn't! He loves you despite your shortcomings. He loves you despite your mistakes. He loves you despite your wrongdoings. He loves you with everything about you in full view. This is what makes His love so unbelievable."

"Likeness, as I listen to you explain Dad's love, I must confess that I don't think I could ever love the way that Dad does."

"You are right. On your own, you will never be able to love like Dad does. However, as my abiding presence begins to influence your soul and you grow in your companionship with Dad, how you think, feel, and act will no longer be solely under your control. Your likeness to Him will take over your soul, and you will find yourself being a vessel through which Dad's love will flow freely. At that point it will no longer be you who lives, but it will be Dad who lives through you! Dad's love will come to its full maturity in you, and the only thing you can do is spread His love to others."

Before I could say anything, Likeness continued. "I know what I am telling you is a lot for you to absorb at one time. So let's end our conversation here and do something a little more fun. Besides, I can show you Dad's love better than I can tell you about His love. As He spoke those words, I saw a twinkle in His eye, and instantly I knew something was about to change.

"Close your eyes," He said.

I did so without hesitation.

Chapter 8

UNCONDITIONAL LOVE IN MOTION

Likeness asked me to open my eyes again. To my amazement, we were seated in a church with hundreds of people about to witness a wedding.

Likeness looked at me and said, "Don't worry. No one knows we are here. We can talk freely."

"Whose wedding is this?"

"You'll see in a minute. All I will tell you is that it is someone you know."

Likeness and I were seated on the front row directly behind the bride and groom, who were standing with their backs to the audience as they faced the minister conducting the wedding. The bride had on a long white-on-white lace dress with an eight-foot flowing train spread out across the floor, making her look like royalty. The embroidery on the dress caused it to sparkle in the light. The groom wore a black tuxedo with tails, a white shirt, and a purple bow tie.

There were three bridesmaids and three groomsmen. The bridesmaids wore the same type of dress as the bride but without the train. The groomsmen all wore the same tuxedos and shirts as the groom but with black bowties. The minister was standing on the steps of the stage and was slightly elevated from the rest of the wedding party. To his right and left were several flower pots filled with lilies and orchids. On the stage behind him were a beautiful black baby grand piano and a set of drums behind a Plexiglas enclosure.

My observations came to an abrupt halt when I heard the minister say, "We have come to the part of the wedding ceremony where the vows are exchanged between the bride and groom. I will do the traditional vows in just a minute, but first I am going to offer the bride and groom an opportunity to share their vows with each other in their own words. It makes their commitment to each other more personal and allows them a chance to share the uniqueness of their love for one another. The bride will go first, followed by the groom."

The bride and groom turned to each other so that the audience could share in their exchange. We were able to see a profile of them both. At first I did not recognize the bride or the groom. I remembered the bride from somewhere, but I couldn't put my finger on exactly where. Then she smiled, and immediately I knew who it was. It was the bag lady!

Likeness was smiling from ear to ear. Before I could say anything, He said, "Yes, that is the young lady you met on the city street. Now pay attention so you can hear what she is about to say."

Several questions were running through my head, but I decided to dismiss them, hoping that they might be answered in what she was about to share.

Struggling to speak with tears running down her cheeks, her hands shaking, and a beautiful smile on her face, she began. "Five years ago, no one could have told me that it was possible for me to be standing at this altar about to get married. Five years ago I was a mental, emotional, and spiritual mess. I was homeless, friendless, and hopeless. I had decided to live the rest of my life in total isolation from anybody and everybody who would try to befriend me. And to make matters worse, I had developed a terrible addiction to alcohol to cover up my pain.

"Then you reentered my life. At first I did everything I could to run and hide from you. I rejected your kindness and your love. I insulted you. I embarrassed you. I did everything I could think of to discourage your love. But you persisted. You would search for me sometimes for days on end. You brought me gifts. You bought me meals. You treated me with respect and dignity even though at the time I lived on the streets. What really amazed me the most is that you wanted to spend time with me. You would sit in the park with me all night long. You loved me unconditionally. I had never experienced love like this before. You were patient, you were kind, and you never allowed anything I did to dissuade your love.

"It is your love that has transformed me. It is your love that has given me hope. Literally it was your love that brought me off the street. It was your love that started me on the path of recovery. It was your love that made me believe in myself again. When I look at my life today, I am amazed at what I see. I haven't had a drink in three years. I am no longer homeless, helpless, or friendless. You have loved me into this moment, and I vow with all of my love to be to you what you have been to me. I will forever be devoted to you and only you. Before God and the people of God I take you to be my husband and I vow to always be your wife."

By this time, there wasn't a dry eye in the church. The minister was crying; the entire wedding party was crying; I heard several people behind me crying; Likeness was crying; and I was crying too!

Likeness commented,"The groom functioned in the likeness of Dad, and today you are witnessing the results! The atmosphere is charged with emotion because Dad's love always touches the hearts of men. It is time to make another stop. There is a reception we must attend."

"A reception? This wedding is not over yet. How can we go to the reception?" As soon as I asked that question, I knew how foolish it was. I had been experiencing the impossible all day long. How could I ask such a silly question?

Likeness said, "I see you have answered your own question."

"Likeness, this mind-reading thing is really weird."

Chapter 9

TAKING THE LIMITS OFF LOVE

Likeness smiled and said, "Look around you. We are already where we need to go."

I saw that we were no longer in the church. We were seated in what appeared to be a ballroom. There was a square-shaped dance floor in the center of the room with the largest crystal chandelier I had ever seen directly above it. Round tables were organized in a semicircle around the dance floor on three sides. The long, straight head table on a slight platform on the fourth side was the focal point of the room. There were eight seats at that table, but no one was seated there. Each table was draped with linen tablecloths and had a five-piece table setting. The plates were made of fine china, and all of the glassware was crystal. At the center of each table was a round cake covered with chocolate icing and an ornament of the bride and groom on top. Several people mingled and talked with one another as classical music played in the background. Once again my observations were interrupted by what happened next.

A gentleman picked up the microphone and said, "Excuse me. May I have everyone's attention please. Can we all start making our way to our seats so we can get on with tonight's festivities? Thank you."

People began to make their way back to their seats. I turned to Likeness, and before I could say anything he said, "I love wedding receptions almost as much as I love weddings."

"Why is that?" I asked, expecting to hear Him say something profound.

"Because I love to see people having fun!"

"That's it?"

"Yes, that's it! I love to see people enjoying one another. It is a simple as that for me."

"I agree. It is good to see people having fun."

I looked at the head table and saw my Korean American friend for the first time. He was sitting at the head table with his Latina wife. I said to myself, "Good for him! He made the decision to marry her after all." Later I learned that seated next to him were His mother and his father and seated next to his bride were her mother and father. At the far end of each side of the table sat the best man and the maid of honor.

I turned to Likeness and said, "I see he made his decision."

"Yes, he did. Now let's see what has happened as a result of the decision he has made."

I turned my attention to the head table just in time to see the best man take the microphone. He said, "At this time we are going to have a toast from the parents of both the bride and the groom. The groom's family will go first, followed by the family of the bride."

As the father stood up, tension seemed to fill the air, or maybe it was just me. I remembered my Korean friend's dilemma. The last time I saw him, he was indecisive about marrying his fiancée because of his parents' stanchly traditional disapproval of marrying someone outside of their nationality. I sat there on edge, hoping that this was not about to be an embarrassing moment for my friend and his bride. I looked over at Likeness, and He just smiled and slightly pointed His finger toward the stage, signaling for me to return my attention there.

The groom's father stood up and faced his son and his son's new bride and began, "Before I make a toast to the newlywed couple, there are a few things that I would like to share with them and our friends and family in attendance. On this special occasion I feel it is fitting to express what this day means for me and my family. Most of you here who know me understand that I am a man of very few words, and when I do speak, I like to get straight to the point. This time, however, what I have to say requires a longer explanation than I would normally offer, so I ask you to please bear with me.

"From the time that my son was a child, my wife and I knew that as we raised him, we wanted him to grow into a young man who displayed four important characteristics. We wanted him to be respectful, resourceful, responsible, and relational. We wanted him to respect his parents, his elders, his family, his friends, and all of mankind. We wanted him to be resourceful enough to earn a living for himself and his family when he left our home. We wanted him to be responsible for his own action and choices. And as far as relationships go, we wanted him to love God and get along well with others. We did our best to instill in him strong Christian values. I stand here today as a proud father. My son displays all of these characteristics and more."

"Whew!" I thought. "This won't be an embarrassing moment after all."

Then the father said, "But there is something I must confess today that I am greatly embarrassed about."

"Uh-oh," I thought. "Maybe I spoke too soon."

He continued, "I have to admit that when my son told me of his plans to marry his wife, I was not happy. I always thought that my son would carry on our family traditions and marry a Korean girl. By the way, if anyone is feeling a little nervous about this, please relax. I have already discussed this with my son, his wife, and her family. After our conversation, we all agreed that what I am about to share needs to be said."

At that point, I almost passed out because of the relief I felt.

"As I said, I wasn't too happy about my son marrying outside of our nationality. For a while, he and I were at odds about his decision. In fact, our relationship became very strained. We had several uncomfortable conversations about his proposed marriage, and I made life very difficult for him. I threatened to disown him, I refused to speak to him, and at times

I just ignored him—all in an attempt to get him to change his mind. But he would not alter his decision. His love for his fiancée caused him to stand his ground. His conviction was strong, and his mind was set.

"During one of our conversations, he asked me a question that completely changed my heart. He asked me how I could let our family traditions put such limits on God's love. He took to me scripture and showed me the unifying power of God's love. I saw that for those of us who have been embraced by the love of Christ, there is no distinction between us. There is neither Jew nor Greek; there is neither slave nor free; there is neither male nor female. We are all one in Christ.

"At first I did not want to accept this truth. I wanted to ignore it. My belief system was too deeply rooted in family tradition. I was so wrapped up in culture that I had completely overlooked Christ. I was more concerned about what other people thought of me than I was about my relationship with God. All I could think about was that I did not want to be a disgrace to my family heritage. In reality, my love for God played second fiddle to my love for country. In my mind, God was Korean."

He paused. You could have heard a pin drop.

"The son I had raised to love God caused me to reexamine my own love, and I discovered I was guilty of loving God on my own terms. I had placed limits on my love for God, my love for family, and my love for friends. I had completely forgotten about God's unlimited love for me. I had completely forgotten that God had given up His son for me so that I could be welcomed freely into His family. If my son had decided to change his decision, I would have never learned this most valuable lesson. I might have lived the rest of my life completely unaware of the limited nature of my love. But because he reflected the image and likeness of God, my love will never be the same again! I am embarrassed to admit this truth about my love, but I hope my honest confession will get all of us to examine our own hearts and in honor of this memorable occasion take the limits off of our love for one another. In the end, all we have is one another, and loving each other well is a great testament to our love for God."

He lifted his champagne glass and said, "And so today when I lift my glass to toast my son and his lovely bride, I do so as a man who has been transformed by the unlimited love of my son and daughter-in-law whom I will fully love and support as husband and wife. May you both enjoy the lifelong fruit of unlimited love for one another!"

The ballroom erupted with thunderous applause. I sat there for a moment just taking it all in. Likeness was still smiling from ear to ear. We both stood up and joined in the applause.

Likeness said, "I think we have seen enough here. We have two other stops to make and we are just in time for..."

"My African American actress friend?" I completed the sentence.

"You got it, Grasshopper! I can't get anything past you," Likeness said with a smile.

"Where are we going?" I asked.

"You are already there. You just haven't noticed it yet."

Chapter 10

THIS LOVE IS UNBELIEVABLE!

When I looked around, sure enough, Likeness and I were no longer in the ballroom. This time we were in an auditorium filled with at least three thousand people. We were still clapping, and so was everyone else around us. In front of us was a beautifully decorated stage with a floor that appeared to be one sheet of black glass. A man and a woman stood at the glass lectern at the center of the stage. Behind them a large, elevated globe was printed with the words "The Seventh Annual International Actors' Awards." On both sides of the globe were flags representing every country in the world.

In the foreground above the stage were two large video screens, each showing an elegant photograph of my African American friend. Above her photograph were the words "The International Actress of the Year." Tears welled up in my eyes, and I clapped even harder. For a brief moment, I felt like a proud father even though I didn't know her well. Then I saw her climbing the stairs of the stage with a male escort. She was even more stunning in person than her picture portrayed.

She wore a long, sky blue strapless silk dress that revealed her sky blue and white shoes in the front but draped all the way to the floor in the back, creating a short train which flowed across the floor. It was tailored to fit her body but it wasn't too tight, and although it was strapless, it was very tasteful. A white chiffon shawl covered her bare shoulders. She had on a classy pearl necklace and a matching pearl bracelet. What amazed me the most was that she had gotten rid of all of the fake stuff I remembered from our first encounter. She didn't have on a wig. Her hair was cut short to fit her face. She didn't have on very much make-up or those long fake fingernails. She looked naturally elegant and beautiful.

As usual, Likeness was grinning from ear to ear. "She has really come into her own, hasn't she?"

"She sure has," I replied.

I knew instinctively that I was about to hear how this miraculous change had come about.

Her escort stepped away and walked off stage. She hugged both of the people standing at the lectern. The woman handed her the trophy and exited the stage along with her male companion. My African American friend looked at the trophy with tears running down her cheeks. She found it hard to compose herself long enough to speak. The audience was patient and very gracious. During her attempt to settle down from the excitement, the crowd clapped and cheered louder. Everyone in the auditorium was standing. Eventually the cheering and clapping tapered off, and she was ready to speak.

"Thank you so much. Thank you. Thank you. Please be seated. I cannot believe that I am standing before you tonight as the recipient of this precious and prestigious award. First I want to thank God for making this moment possible for me. I also want to thank all of you who voted for me as International Actress of the Year. It is truly an honor to be standing here, especially when I consider all of the other wonderful international actresses whom I love and admire.

"I thank everybody at Agape Movie Studios who worked feverishly to make every movie I acted in such a great learning experience. It is literally impossible for me to individually name all of the people who made this moment possible, so I am not going to run the risk of forgetting one or two names. I will simply say thank you to our entire Agape family. All of you know my heart and know that I love you all very much. What is so amazing about all of my family at Agape Movie

Studios is that we have created such a humble, loving environment that most of the people I would name would be embarrassed by the attention.

"We all know that what we have at Agape wouldn't be possible without the love and vision of one man—our founder and CEO, whose motto has always been to allow God's love to reign supreme. Because of the vision of this great man, I stand here as someone who has been completely change by his love. I want everyone here to understand that when I say that I am changed I am not referring only to my acting skills and abilities, although I am sure I have grown as an actress. I am referring to my personhood.

"When I came to Agape Movie Studios over three years ago I was a wreck. I had low self-esteem. I saw myself through the eyes of other people. I was cynical. I hid behind anything I could find to hide behind: make-up, clothing, wigs, jewelry, blame, shame—you name it. I was very guarded. I was bitter. I was angry and extremely negative. I had no idea who I was or what I truly wanted out of life. I imagine I wasn't a very pleasant person to be around. I had allowed life to take its toll on me.

"At my first audition I met our founder and CEO. He told me that my audition wasn't very good, but he believed that I could do better. So he invited me to return for what I thought would be a second audition. To my surprise it wasn't an audition at all. Instead, he wanted to get to know more about me as a person. At first I couldn't believe it, especially in light of the fact that he paid me such a wonderful salary to do so. But it was true. He asked me questions about myself that no one has ever asked me, and I talked to him about things I had never discussed with anyone. I revealed hidden secrets, mistakes, and struggles. I shared my dreams, aspirations, and hopes with him. What amazed me the most was that the more he learned about me, the kinder he became. Instead of growing cold and distant, he treated me with love and respect. He made me feel special. He made me feel like I was the only one who mattered to him. He was never inappropriate, nor did we develop a romantic relationship. He shared with me the love of God like no one else I had ever met.

"His love radically transformed my life. Please pardon the expression, but He literally loved the hell right out of me! He has loved me into greatness. As I grew to know him, I found out that he treated everyone the same way. Not only does he model such an unbelievable love, but he also teaches others to do so as well. Thus he has created an organization that has experienced one success after another. I stand here as a product of what he created. Agape is more than just the name of our studio; it is our way of life. I stand here as a testimony of the culture he has created. I dedicate this award to him and my entire Agape family. With his permission I would like to place this prestigious award in the front foyer of our studio offices along with all of the other magnificent awards our family has earned over the years. Thank you all so much!"

The crowd once again stood with cheers and applause. She waved and blew kisses with both hands, and the clapping and cheering continued.

Likeness and I stood up with the rest of the crowd.

"I am really proud of her!" I exclaimed.

Likeness replied, "I am proud of her too!"

"Who is the founder and CEO? He sounds like a really great guy!"

"Let's just call him a Likeness representative."

"I like that—a Likeness representative," I repeated.

"He is really a phenomenal man who lives his life with a clear understanding of who he is and what he is created to do," Likeness said.

"I would really like to meet him. It seems he has really mastered this likeness thing."

"No, he hasn't mastered it; it has mastered him! He has just surrendered himself to Dad, and Dad has done the rest. And as far as meeting him is concerned, you have already met him."

"When did I meet him?"

"Whom haven't you seen already?"

"Whom haven't I seen already? Oh...don't tell me you are referring to the rich guy I met in the big city!"

"Okay. I won't tell you."

"I can't believe it!"

"You can't believe what?"

"I can't believe that the rich guy is the founder and CEO of Agape Movie Studios. I have got to see this because he was such a..."

"Remember, you can't always judge a book by its cover," Likeness interrupted.

"Yeah, I guess you are right. But the person the actress described doesn't share even a faint resemblance to the man I remember."

"Well, let's see. I hope you are ready for this!"

"You hope I am ready for what?"

"You'll see, my friend. You will see."

"Oh, Lord. Not again..."

Chapter 11

Unusual Is What Unusual Does

The next thing I knew, Likeness and I were standing in a banquet hall. Immediately I noticed that it was a black-tie affair. All of the men were dressed in tuxedos with black bow ties, and all of the women were adorned in gorgeous evening gowns. The banquet hall was set up in a way that resembled the wedding reception of my Korean American friend except that there was no dance floor or large chandelier in the center of the room. Instead there were round tables spread out throughout the entire hall. Each table was covered with a white linen tablecloth. Everyone had finished the main course, and the servers were pouring coffee and serving dessert. I could smell the freshly brewed coffee along with the aroma of leftover food being collected by the banquet staff.

It was an intimate setting of no more than three hundred people. The room was filled with the sounds of people conversing with one another and jazz music playing softly in the background. There were no banners or printed programs anywhere, so I didn't know what to expect. There was a lectern with a microphone on a short platform near the central wall in the room. From my conversation with Likeness, I assumed that the banquet was organized to honor the founder and CEO of Agape Movie Studios.

I turned to Likeness and asked, "What type of gathering is this?"

"You will find out in just a minute."

Just as Likeness finished his response, I saw something that completely threw me off guard. Seated near the platform at a single table were the bag lady and her husband, the Korean American and his Latina wife, the African American actress, the rich man and a woman I did not know and his chauffeur. Seeing them all together caused several questions to start running through my head: Why are they all here? How are they connected to each other? What in the world is the chauffeur doing up there? What happened to the rich man that caused him to change so drastically? Who is that woman sitting next to the rich man?

Likeness said, "I know you have several questions floating around in your head. All of them are going to be answered in just a few minutes."

At that very moment the rich man got up from the table and walked over to the platform. He adjusted the microphone, raised a small bell, and shook it a few times in front of the microphone. Then he said, "Ladies and gentlemen, may I have your attention please."

The conversations began to taper off slowly until it was apparent that all eyes were on him.

He continued, "Thank you very much. As you all know, I have been designated to help close out this awesome evening. I tell you what, thanks to our wonderful host, this has truly been a magnificent night! Don't you agree?"

Immediately everyone stood and began to cheer and applaud. The rich man applauded too. I saw several people hugging each other and several high fives being exchanged. Eventually the joyful response tapered off, and everyone returned to their seats.

He continued, "Tonight's Agape Celebration has truly been a night to remember. The amazing stories of love we have heard have made us laugh and made us cry. They have challenged us, and I am sure that they have permanently transformed our lives. To all of those who shared their stories, we thank you for giving us the pleasure of sharing this intimate moment with you."

Once again the room erupted in applause. A few people stood and cheered again.

I felt like I had missed something important, but I quickly dismissed the notion since I knew that Likeness's timing was perfect. I concluded that what I needed to learn had yet to unfold, so I held my peace.

The rich man continued, "This annual celebration is just another reminder that for Agape Movie Studios, agape is more than just a name—it is a lifestyle! For me to be a part of a celebration like this is truly remarkable. I never would have thought in a million years that I would ever be involved in a celebration of love. At one time in my life, not too long ago, I was very cold and callous. Instead of getting involved in meaningful relationships, I poured myself into my work. As a result of my hard work, I amassed a sizable fortune. However, the cost of that fortune was immense. I became so obsessed with accumulating wealth that I completely destroyed several relationships in the process.

"I had a failed marriage that ended in divorce. I had a son who barely knew me. I had two parents whom I seldom called and never visited. I had my only brother who worked for me but was more like an employee than a blood relative. At one point in my life, I didn't know if I possessed my possessions or if my possessions possessed me. My identity was lost in what I possessed. The more I had, the more superior I felt. I couldn't enjoy any genuine relationships because I thought all anybody ever wanted from me was my money. I became very paranoid and trusted no one. I am ashamed to admit it, but I looked down on anyone who did not have as much wealth as I did.

"The sad part was that I had no one to share my good fortune with. I was a miserably lonely man. On the surface, I am sure it appeared to those around me that I was a man of wealth and power, but the reality was quite different. The truth was that I was buried beneath everything I owned. I didn't know who I truly was or what I was created to do. On the outside it looked like my life was full, but on the inside I felt quite empty.

"All of that changed when I met my chauffeur. As soon as I met him, I could tell there was something unusual about him. As I expected of a chauffeur, he was very polite and accommodating. But he had an uncanny ability to know what I needed—sometimes even before I knew it. I will never forget how he got my secretary to provide him with information about my family's birthdates and any other special celebrations so that he could send gifts on my behalf. He arranged a schedule with my housekeeper so that he could drop off my dry cleaning so that I wouldn't have to worry about my clothes. He always had the limo equipped with my favorite reading material. What made all of this so special was that none of these things were a part of his job description.

"I have to admit, at first I thought he was up to something. I was really suspicious of his unusual behavior. But as I got to know him, I saw that his efforts were genuine. As a result of his overwhelming kindness, he and I began to develop a much more meaningful relationship. In a very short time, he went from being one of my employees to becoming a confidant and friend. He always had a listening ear, and the wisdom that he shared with me was inspirational and insightful. Because of his wisdom, my wife and I are dating again; my son and I have reconciled our relationship; my parents are now an integral part of my life; and my brother has become one of my closest friends."

Once again the joyful noise of clapping and cheering filled the room. Eventually he continued. "As a result of his uncanny wisdom, I offered him a much more prestigious position in my company. He refused. When he did so I really thought he was unusual."

Several people laughed, and the rich man chuckled too. I wasn't sure why this comment was funny. Maybe it was an inside joke.

The rich man went on. "He told me that he was satisfied with being my chauffeur. I found his response to be odd, but I accepted his decision. Here was a man who served me well and didn't want anything more in return. On their own merit, his friendship and wisdom alone were enough to get me to begin to view life differently. The next thing I discovered about this man, however, not only took me by surprise; it radically changed my life forever. In fact, what I discovered is the single most important reason why I am standing before you at this very moment. I discovered that my chauffeur was not a chauffeur after all, but he was and is the founder and CEO of Agape Movie Studios! I also discovered that over the years he has worked as a janitor, a construction worker, a cook, and a corporate executive—all in the name of touching different people's lives with the agape of God.

"Everyone in this room has been affected by the love of God that flows through this man. He has dedicated his life to sharing God's love with as many people as he can. When I asked him what made him take the job as my chauffeur, his reply was simple. He said it was agape. I stand before you today because I have been deeply touched by the love of a man who understands what it means to live his life in the image and likeness of God. Like all of you at this festive occasion, I feel like I have been touched by an angel. Ladies and gentlemen, I proudly present to you my brother and closest friend, the founder and CEO of Agape Movie Studios!"

The place erupted with a standing ovation.

I was floored! I couldn't believe it! The chauffeur?...The chauffeur was the founder and CEO of Agape Movies Studios?

While the cheering was still going on, I turned to Likeness and said, "I thought you told me that the rich man was the founder and CEO."

"No. You drew that conclusion on your own. I simply asked you whom you hadn't seen already. And you said, 'Don't tell me it is the rich man.' I agreed with your request and said 'Okay, I won't tell you.'"

"You are right! You didn't tell me the rich man was the CEO. I concluded that on my own. But I would have never guessed that it was the chauffeur. He seemed so insignificant to what you wanted me to learn."

"That is how Dad works. He doesn't always use the 'important people.' He loves to use ordinary people to do extraordinary things."

"Wow! I am blown away! "

"I understand. But always remember and never forget: Anybody can do what has been done through this man. The power is not in the man. The power is in what flows through the man. Dad will always give to you what he knows will flow through you!"

"I guess all it takes is one committed person to affect the lives of many."

"You are right. That is what I wanted you to see. Any man or woman who truly understands what it means to live in the image and likeness of Dad can make a lasting impact in this world!"

I didn't notice what was happening around us as we talked, but the next thing I knew, we were back in the place where our journey began.

Chapter 12

LIVING IN HIS LIKENESS

Once again I was in my bathrobe, and Likeness was in the mirror. Two things were different. First, the room seemed brighter than before. I remembered Likeness telling me that the brightness of the room was a sign of Dad bringing me into a greater spiritual awareness. Second, Likeness's appearance had changed. He looked a little more translucent.

Likeness was standing directly in front of me, looking just like me, except for His translucent glow. We carried on the rest of our conversation face to face.

I felt a sadness come over me because I sensed that our time together was about to come to an end. I decided to ask a few questions about the founder and CEO of Agape Movie Studios that were still roaming around in my mind.

"Likeness, I still have a few questions about my friends."

"I know you do. You want to know how everyone was connected. Well, the bag lady's husband works for AMS. When he broke his fiancée's heart, he went to the founder and explained the terrible incident that took place between him and the bag lady. At that time the husband was so devastated by his own behavior that he went through a period of deep depression. The founder loved him back to life, then coached him into reconciling with the bag lady. The founder mentored the husband every step of the way through the reconciliation. You didn't notice it at the time, but the founder was the best man in their wedding. That is how he was connected to the bag lady and her husband."

"Now that you mention it, I do remember seeing him in the wedding!"

"As far as the Korean American and his Latina wife are concerned, the founder attends the same church they attend and mentored the Korean American through his challenge with his parents. At one point, the Korean American was about to call off the wedding altogether and try to get over his love for his bride-to-be. He had concluded that the problem between him, his fiancée, and his family was too much for him to bear. But the founder talked him out of doing so. The founder assured him that love would prevail in the end of his challenging situation, and it did. You already know the African American actress's story and how she is connected to the founder."

"Yes, but I want to know how the founder happened to be introduced to the rich man."

"I am getting there. The founder was introduced to the rich man through the rich man's wife. Shortly after her divorce, she took a job at AMS. As is the custom at AMS, the founder got to know her and discovered her undying love for her husband. He got her permission to get involved to see if reconciliation was a possibility and started moonlighting as a chauffeur for the rich man. You heard the rest. The unknown woman seated at the table with the rest of them was the rich man's ex-wife, soon to be his wife again."

"Oh, what a tangled web we weave!" I replied.

Likeness responded, "This is a simple web. Try unraveling a web that spans across generations. You haven't seen a web until you see a generational one!"

"This one is enough for me. I can't begin to imagine what a generational web looks like."

We shared a brief smile, then the mood became serious once again.

Likeness said, "I am starting to see more of Dad in you. With everything you have learned, you are now ready to do even greater things than the founder has done. But there is one more thing that I must draw your attention to."

"What is that?"

"It is the importance of forgiveness. If you want to live effectively in Dad's likeness, the love you share with others must be saturated with forgiveness."

"I am glad that you mentioned forgiveness because I noticed that it played a big part in just about everybody's story."

"No, forgiveness was a part of everyone's story."

"I can see forgiveness at work between the bag lady and her husband. I can also see it between the Korean American and his parents. And certainly it is present between the rich man and his wife-to-be. But who did the African American actress have to forgive?"

"She had to forgive herself. At one time in her life, she hated herself. In order for her to accept herself for who she is, she had to forgive herself first."

"Wow! I never thought of that."

"Yes, self-forgiveness is as important as forgiving others. Sometimes it is more important. Countless people are stuck in a rut because they have refused to forgive themselves for something that they have done. Self-unforgiveness is very toxic!"

"What else do I need to know about forgiveness?"

"If you are going to truly understand the importance of forgiveness, the first thing you need to know is that Dad has made each of us perfectly imperfect."

"What do you mean by 'perfectly imperfect'?"

"Our imperfections are a part of Dad's perfect plan. If we were all perfect, we would always make the right decisions, we would always have the right answers, and we would always do the right thing. Essentially, we would have no need of anyone. We wouldn't need each other, nor would we need Dad. We would never have to be taught anything, nor would there be any occasion to learn. We would never make any errors or mistakes. We would be self-sufficient, and every man and woman would be an island unto himself or herself.

"To prevent this type of isolation and to promote a sense of family, Dad in His great wisdom made us perfectly imperfect. Our imperfections are designed to get us to depend on one another. Dad takes two perfectly imperfect people and puts them together to make a perfect situation. Only Dad can do that. As a matter of fact, taking two imperfect people and making a perfect situation can't happen without Dad.

"Because our imperfection makes us susceptible to error, we are constantly in need of forgiveness. It doesn't matter if you are a cute little child or a cranky old man. Everyone needs to be forgiven for something.

"Some people hurt others intentionally and some unintentionally. Some pain is considered major, and some pain is considered minor. Either way, the fact remains: Forgiveness is necessary if we are ever going to get along in this world. Forgiveness is so important to Dad that He determines His forgiveness for us by how well we are able to forgive one another. As a matter of fact, Dad is so serious about forgiveness that He doesn't want us to do anything for Him until we forgive one another."

"It is scary to think that Dad determines His forgiveness for us based on our forgiveness of one another. That's something to think about."

"Yes, it is. Especially since unforgiveness is considered poison in Dad's family. It is the number one cause of disunity among Dad's children. Unforgiveness completely destroys relationships, and relationships are Dad's biggest priority."

"When it comes to forgiveness, where do we begin?"

"You begin with making a decision to forgive. Forgiveness is a choice. It is not necessarily emotional. In fact, it is mental before it becomes emotional. It has nothing to do with other people. It doesn't matter if they see the error of their ways or not. It also doesn't matter if they desire or deserve to be forgiven or not. What matters is that you are willing and able to forgive. It is about you deciding to guard your heart from being controlled by the action or inaction of others. When you carry unforgiveness in your heart, it hurts you more than it does the other person. It takes away your peace. It robs you of your joy. It hardens your heart and ultimately restricts the flow of love in your life."

"But forgiveness is not always easy," I countered.

"Yes, I know. At times, it is almost impossible. But hard or not, it is necessary if you are going to live in the Likeness of Dad. He specializes in forgiveness. All of mankind would be doomed if He wasn't a forgiving Dad."

"Why do you think people have such a hard time with forgiveness?"

"There are several reasons, but I'll tell you four of the more common ones. The first reason is *denial*. Most people live in denial about themselves. Whenever they think about themselves, they deny their own need to be forgiven for some of the terrible things they have done to others. They compare their wrong to the wrong of others, and of course the wrong of others always seems worse than their own. Most people are quick to forgive their own offenses because they feel they had a 'legitimate' reason to do what they did. But when it comes to others, their standards are different. Simply put, they have a hard time forgiving others because they fail to realize their own shortcomings.

"The second reason forgiveness is so hard is the *devastation* of the pain associated with the offense. Anything that causes pain is hard to get over. When pain is present, the last thing you think of is forgiveness. In most instances, pain causes you to want revenge. You want the other person to hurt as much as you do. But here is what is interesting about revenge: It never takes away the pain you feel. It only perpetuates the pain. Two wrongs never make things right.

"The third reason is *doubt*. Most people fail to forgive because they doubt Dad's ability to heal them of their pain. Make no mistake about it: I realize how difficult forgiveness can be, but whenever Dad gets involved, nothing is impossible. He doesn't necessarily remove the memory of the pain, but He strengthens you enough to convert the pain to passion. Then your passion becomes compassion, and you find yourself on the other side of pain helping others. Always remember and never forget Dad never wastes a hurt. He has an uncanny way of changing pain into purpose."

Then Likeness asked me a series of questions that really caused me to pause and think. "Whenever you forgive someone for something, why do you forgive them? Do you forgive them for yourself? Do you forgive them for them? Do you forgive them for Dad?"

"Uh, I am not really sure...I would have to say I forgive them for my own sake."

"That is why most people forgive others. They do it for themselves. That is the fourth reason why forgiveness is so hard for people. They *don't forgive for the right reason*. They make it about them, or they make it about the other person. The primary reason to forgive others is to please Dad. When you forgive others for Dad, it places His principles above your problems. At that point, you really recognize that Dad is more important than anything else in your life."

"Likeness, you have certainly given me a lot of food for thought. Your explanation of forgiveness has given me a better understanding of its importance and leaves no room for doubt. I can't say that I don't know where to begin because you have given me a thorough road map to follow. I know that as a result of this encounter, my life will never be the same."

"I am overjoyed to hear those words. I have accomplished my initial assignment. I want to leave you with something else to think about before I go.

"Can you imagine a world without poverty? Can you imagine a world without hatred and division? Can you imagine a world without separation and divorce? Can you imagine a world of an abundance of love for everyone? Does this sound too good to be true? It almost sounds like heaven doesn't it? Well, it is. And guess what? That is why you have been created. You have been created to establish heaven right here on earth. That has been Dad's plan from the very beginning. If you can't imagine such a world, then the world is in deep trouble. Because you can only create a world that you can imagine. Always remember and never forget: You have been given dominion, and therefore, you can create anything you want to create. Dad has placed His hope in you and the decision to live in His likeness is in your hands.

"Likeness, I will do whatever it takes."

"I know you will. That is why Dad sent me to you. You have a heart to live in His likeness."

Once again sadness started to overcome me as I sensed our time together coming to an end. But there was one more question I had to ask. "A minute ago, you mentioned that this was your initial assignment. Does that mean I will see you again?"

"You will see me every time you look in the mirror. I am you, remember?" He smiled.

"Yeah, yeah, I know. But you know what I mean. Will we ever talk again?"

"Let me put it this way. Dad only continues to give wisdom to those who use it. He is not into wasting words or wisdom. If you use the wisdom I have given you, I am sure I will talk with you again. That choice is yours too."

Likeness continued, " Do you remember your notebook?

"Yes, I do."

I saw it lying on the marble countertop in front of me next to the purple pen. I reached for the book and placed my right hand on top of it.

Likeness said solemnly, "Do you swear to tell the truth, the whole truth, and nothing but the truth so help you Dad?"

"What did you say?"

"Sorry—I couldn't resist the humor. When I saw you reach for the book and put your right hand on it, I thought we were about to do a swearing-in ceremony."

We both burst out laughing.

I said, "Likeness, you are funnnnny!"

We chuckled a few more times, and Likeness continued talking. "The notebook has a complete record of everything that has happened between us. Use it to share this message with the rest of the world. Your assignment is to spread this story with as many people as you can. There is no way for you to do everything that needs to be done on your own. If you follow my instructions, you are sure to see remarkable results. You have everything you need to get started.

"Don't delay. Do it today. And rest assured, every time you look in the mirror, I will be watching you. Until we meet again, always remember and never forget: I am only a likeness away."

AFTERWORD

I sincerely hope that you enjoyed reading this book as much as I enjoyed writing it. Frankly, I am still amazed that God entrusted me with the task of doing so. Make no mistake about it: God was my motivation and inspiration throughout the entire process.

In fact, I remember the day I began writing the book. It started as a loving request. The Lord said to me, "I have something to tell you. I want you to sit down and write," and I did. The moment I sat down at my computer, He began to direct and guide me through the story. I would type as long as He would speak. When He stopped speaking, I would stop writing.

There were times when I didn't know where the story was going, which made the writing process very uncomfortable. But time and time again, He would give me further instructions that enabled me to feel more comfortable with the progress of the book. I had to learn to "lose control" and trust Him to help me complete the work. There were times when I was frustrated and wanted to give up. But He wouldn't let me. He would provide me with a specific insight or memory that would spark my interest again.

Writing the book changed my view of God, myself, and others. Prior to writing this book I viewed God as an almighty, all-knowing, all-present God who would bless me if I did right and punish me if I did wrong. But this book has taught me that God takes no delight in punishing me for the wrong I have done. The wrong I have done carries with it its own punishment. God is more interested in loving the hell out of me than punishing me for the hell I have caused. His desire is to be my Dad. He is a loving parent who wants the best for me. In fact, He views us all as one big family, and He wants the best for us all.

I also learned that regardless of what I do, I will forever carry the image of my Dad. I am His son, and nothing can ever change that truth! My reflection in the mirror now serves as a reminder to me that there is more to me than meets the eye. My true identity is in how I live on the inside, not in how I look on the outside. Writing this book has enabled me to fully embrace the fact that I have been given the gift of choice and that my love is demonstrated in the choices I make.

Finally, this book helped me to see others differently. It brought me face to face with my own prejudices, judgments, and criticism of others. I have begun to erase racial, cultural, and class distinctions from my life. I have gained a deeper appreciation for the preciousness of every person I meet regardless of their situation or station in life. My sole responsibility is to be a Likeness representative and allow Dad's love to flow through me.

This book is contagious! Just as it has affected and infected me, I sincerely hope it does the same for you and everybody you know. Let's tell everyone we know about it—the world will be glad we did!

Terry

Appendix

MAKING A LIFE-AFFIRMING CHOICE

In this book, Likeness has revealed Dad's heart for all of us. His heart's desire is that we love Him with all of our heart, soul, and mind. Dad wants us all to be in a loving relationship with Him. With this in mind, I want to ask you to make a decision today—a decision that will change your life forever.

Perhaps you have never given your heart to the Lord. Chances are you can think of a number of reasons why you haven't. Maybe for the first time you realize that you have been guilty of violating Dad's family values. But here is something you need to understand: No one qualifies on their own merit. But Dad's Family Book of Wisdom says that if you repent by turning away from your wrongdoing and return to Dad, He will forgive you because of the sacrifice of our Older Brother on the cross. Dad made the ultimate sacrifice to afford us the opportunity to return back to Him. If you are willing to make that choice today, please pray this simple prayer:

> *Dad, I am sorry. I really see how wrong I have been. I have tried to live my life without You. I have broken every one of Your family values, and my heart is deeply saddened by what I have done. But today I make a decision to acknowledge the wonderful sacrifice that You have made for me. I confess with my mouth and believe in my heart that Christ died for all the wrong I have*

> *done. I also confess that He rose again with all power, making it possible for me to be reconciled in to companionship with You as my loving father. I thank you, Dad, for Your love and acceptance. Amen.*

If you prayed that prayer, *congratulations*—you have just begun a new life! (Do me a favor: Write me an email at **testimonies@ imagetolikeness.com** and let me know you have become a part of Dad's family. It would really lift my spirits to celebrate with you.)

If you are already a believer, maybe Dad has spoken to your heart through the pages of this book. Perhaps you are sensing a strong desire to improve your companionship with Him. Maybe that means getting back into the Word or improving your prayer life. Or maybe you need to get back into fellowship with other believers by attending a local church. Whatever you sense Dad moving you to do, make a decision today to begin—be obedient to His call. Don't put it off until tomorrow. Do it today! If you truly sense Dad drawing you back into companionship with Him, please say this simple prayer:

> *Dad, I am ready to come home. I am tired of trying to live my life without You. I do not want to continue to carry the responsibility of life on my own. Today I rededicate my life to You. I make a conscious decision today to walk away from anything that hinders our relationship. Thank You for making a way for me to return to You. It feels so good to finally come back home. Amen.*

Whatever activity or discipline you decide to do, plan to continue it for at least forty-two days. By then it will become a habit, and you'll be able to incorporate it into your lifestyle. (I ask you to do the same favor for me: Write me an email at **testimonies@imagetolikeness.com** and let me know what you have decided to do. Sharing your decision with me will bring me great delight.)

I pray that all of you will enjoy Dad's choicest blessings!

Message for Facebook Family and Friends

HELP US CHANGE THE WORLD

Now that you have read this book, I know you have an overwhelming sense of Dad's uncommon and unconditional love for you. I am also convinced that just as the message of this story has affected us both, it can also have a wonderful lasting impact on others we know. With this being said, I am asking you to take two immediate actions: First, log on to my website at www.imagetolikeness.com, click on the Facebook link and partner with me by sharing a few lines about how this book has helped you. Second, go to your Facebook page and recommend this book to your Facebook family and friends. Whatever you do, please don't give the story line away. (We don't want to spoil the impact of the book).

Thank you for helping us to change the world!

The i2L Challenge

My i2L team and I are convinced that there are many people in the world today who love Dad and have truly committed themselves to living in His image and likeness. We are also convinced that a lot of these wonderful people are grossly overlooked and therefore never receive the recognition they deserve. These "Image to Likeness" people understand what it means to love Dad and His people.

We want to partner with you to make these people known to the rest of the world. Here is what we propose: If you know of someone who truly exemplifies what it means to live in the image and likeness of Dad, we want to hear their story.

The criteria are simple. They should be faithful in their devotion to Dad, and have an extraordinary heart for loving others. If you know of such a person, go to our website **www.imagetolikeness.com** and tell us about them. Just click on the i2L Challenge icon and follow the prompts. Every month we will select one of the stories submitted and place the winner on our Wall of Fame!

Acknowledgments

As always, I give all praise and thanks to my Lord and Savior Jesus Christ who continues to bless me exceedingly and abundantly above anything I could ever ask or think. This book would not have been possible without His involvement. In fact, He is the real author. He just happened to choose me to write the book.

There are so many wonderful people that I must acknowledge and thank for helping me to finish this work. First there is my darling wife, Joye. As I stated on the dedication page, she is and always has been my greatest supporter. Without her in my life, I doubt very seriously that I would have ever accomplished many of the goals I have set in my life. I initially wrote this book as a surprise for her birthday. When she read the initial manuscript and told me that she thought it was brilliant, I knew that I was on the right path. Sweetheart, thank you for loving me the way you do.

Then there is Melvin M. Maxwell, affectionately known as Max. He was among the first to read the initial manuscript. His words of encouragement and support gave me the assurance I needed to continue writing this book. Max, thank you for the countless conversations and the many hours you spent helping me to complete this project. Your friendship kept me focused on the task at hand.

Dr. Dwight McKinney's timeless wisdom broadened my thinking every time we talked. He was also among the first to read the initial manuscript. His constructive criticism gave me insights that were vital to the flow of the book. Dwight, you have truly been a friend that sticks closer than a brother. Thank you for listening, editing, and commenting on this project.

Next there is Adriane Wise who was introduced to this project by Max. She was our first "reader." She liked the manuscript so much that she decided to become a part of our team. From that moment on, she has worked diligently to help me complete this work. She has read and reread, edited and researched, brainstormed and listened to ideas. She has become a vital part of our book team. Adriane, you have been a breath of fresh air. Your critical eye has helped me to become a better writer. I thank you for adding value to this work with your creativity and expertise.

Theresa Gilmore was also a valuable contributor to the completion of this book. Theresa is the best administrator on the planet! She helped me to get the book ready for my wife's birthday. She enlisted the help of one of my spiritual daughters, Caroline Jones, who actually came up with an idea for the initial cover of the book. Thank you Caroline! Theresa, I thank you for your hard work and dedication. You always do everything you can to help my wife and I succeed. We are eternally grateful for all you do.

Toby Hunter was our second "reader." Toby, I thank you for your honest comments, which added a new dimension to this work. Melody M. Miller (M3) was my graphic designer. Melody is sensational! She worked tirelessly to come up with a cover for this book. She was more than reasonable to work with, and she became a vital part of our book team. Melody, you are the greatest!

Another contributor is Tracey Ruckman. Tracey came highly recommended by another author who enjoyed working with her. Although we have only communicated via e-mail, she was the first official editor to work on my manuscript. Her comments and corrections took my writing to a new level. I especially appreciated her words of encouragement at various places throughout the manuscript. Tracey, I thank you for helping me to improve my written communication skills.

Yet another voice in this magnificent work is Mary Jo Tate. Mary Jo is a dynamo! She is a great editor. Early on in the development of this book, she provided me some suggestions, comments, and writing insights that helped me to fine-tune my thinking about this book. Throughout the entire process, she respected my voice, while at the same time helping me to improve my communication skills. It was apparent from the very beginning that she was going to do her best to make this book an overwhelming success. Mary Jo, you are a precious gift to the literary world!

There are several other people who may not have had any direct involvement with this book but who have greatly contributed to my overall growth and development as a man. My lovely children—Marcus, Joy, Alifah, Ahavah, and Uriel—are my pride and joy. They have been a constant inspiration to me. Daddy loves you all!

Bishop T. Anthony Bronner has been a spiritual father and mentor to me for the past sixteen years. Bishop, if it had not been for your love during my very dark days, none of this would be possible. You loved me into greatness, and for that I am eternally grateful!

Arthur Boyd has been my friend and mentor for sixteen years. He is the older brother I never had. Boyd, I thank you for believing in me when no one else would. You have always been my hero!

There is no way I can leave out my cousin Herb Jones. Herb has literally given me the shirt off his back. Herb, I thank you for you love and support. You helped me out at a time in my life that made it possible for me to become the man that I am.

Eric Gladney is another man whom I have deeply loved for several years. Eric is the godfather to my children and has always been such an inspiration to me. Eric, I thank you for being someone who is always consistent. You are a great man and a wonderful friend.

Ted Howard has been praying for me for years. Ted and I grew up in ministry together. He has an extraordinary prayer life. Ted, thank you for your prayers and words of encouragement. Your prophetic voice has always kept me on the right track.

I dare not forget my beloved spiritual brother and friend, Dr. Kelvin S. Bryant. Kelvin is a covenant brother who will always have a special place in my heart. Time and time again he has demonstrated his commitment to our friendship and spiritual journey together. Kelvin, I thank you for being one of my closest friends.

Another great spirit is Pastor Cliff Lovick. Pastor Lovick is a very dear friend. He has contributed greatly to my devotional life. Cliff, I thank you for encouraging me to go deeper into my companionship with God.

I also want to share my love with my brothers and sister; Duane, Deadra, and Keith. I love each one of you with my whole heart!

Last but not least I want to thank all of the saints of Elim Christian Fellowship in Buffalo, New York, and Greensboro, North Carolina. My wife and I deeply love you all. We thank you for believing in us!

Certainly whenever individuals are singled out in acknowledgments, there is always the possibility to forget other significant people, so to all of those whom I have not mentioned, please charge it to my head and not to my heart.

Thanks to all of you!

About the Author

Terry E. Warr was born in Buffalo, New York, and educated at Hampton University in Hampton, Virginia, where he earned his B.S. in Business Management. Shortly after graduating, he decided to become an international entrepreneur. After spending ten years managing businesses from the continent of Africa back to his home in the United States, Terry has learned that despite cultural, geographical, socio-economic or racial differences, fundamentally three factors unite us all. He believes, "We all share the same fears; we all cry the same tears; and we all die...in so many years."

Along with his multilingual ability, his international business experience has caused him to develop a passion for leadership development. He currently teaches professional, civic, and religious organizations, drawing from the wealth of his experience and exposure. Terry is dedicated to bringing out the best in everyone he meets. He considers himself a pastor-preneur. His greatest reward comes from helping people grow.

In 2000 Terry earned a Master in Divinity from Colgate Rochester Divinity School. He currently serves as the Sr. Pastor of Elim Christian Fellowship in Greensboro, NC.

Terry and his wife Joye reside in High Point, NC. Together they parent five children: Marcus, Joy, Alifah, Ahavah and Uriel.

Manufactured By: RR Donnelley
Momence, IL USA
July , 2010